Plane Truths
for
Living

By John C. Rollins

Plane Truths for Living
Author: John C. Rollins
Published by Austin Brothers Publishing, Fort Worth, Texas
www.abpbooks.com

ISBN 978-0-9983071-8-3
Copyright © 2017 by John C. Rollins

ALL RIGHTS RESERVED. *No part of this book may be reproduced in any form without permission in writing from the publisher, except in the case of brief quotations embodied in critical reviews or articles.*

Unless otherwise noted, verses are taken from the Holy Bible: New International Version, Copyright* 1973, 1978, 1984 by International Bible Society.

Verses identified as (KJV) are taken from the King James Version of the Bible

Note: *The Stanley tools mentioned in this text were manufactured over 50 years ago (the Stanley Bedrock brand was made approximately 100 years ago). Stanley does still produce a newer line of hand planes. The Fulton and Sargent tool companies no longer make hand planes and have not done so for approximately 50 years.*

This and other books published by Austin Brothers Publishing can be purchased at www.abpbooks.com.

Printed in the United States of America
2017 -- First Edition

Every valley shall be exalted, and every mountain and hill shall be made low; and the crooked shall be made straight and the rough places plain.

Isaiah 40:4 KJV

Contents

Acknowledgments	1
Preface	3
Introduction	7
Stopping to Smell the Roses	13
Wood Planes - What Makes Them Special?	17
And The Rough Places Plain	23
Being Content	37
Life Is Temporary	45
What Does Age Have to Do with It?	53
Getting in Tune	59
How Sharp Is Your Blade?	67
What Is Your Blade Made Of?	75
Where the Blade Meets the Wood	83
Got Something "Stuck in Your Craw?"	91
The Angle and Direction of Attack Is Important	99
Collectible versus Usable	107
Analysis Paralysis or the Fear Factor	117
Power Made Perfect in Weakness	125
Being Filled	137
Do Others See Jesus in You?	149
Live Life with a Sense of Purpose	157
Conclusion	163
Post Script	173
John C. Rollins - Biography	179

Acknowledgments

I want to thank the following individuals for their encouragement and assistance during the writing of this book. My first thanks go to Bryan McAnally for his initial guidance and help to get me started. Virginia Reedy, where would I be without your support in the original manuscript? You see, engineers sometimes have difficulty with verb tenses, and active and passive voice and Virginia helped me through many of those hurdles.

Gracie Malone, without you this book would still be languishing in my computer. I cannot thank you enough for your support, encouragement, and willingness to help a new writer understand what it takes to get his book into print. My pastors over the past few years that have taken the time to read, encourage, and make suggestions.

My wife Dee, thanks for putting up with the time alone while I was staring at a computer screen and keyboard, and for pointing out when a section needed additional explanation or simply did not make sense, and to Dee's sister Marian thank you for your comments on the final read through.

Many thanks to my men's study group (Hutch, Wade, Joel, Bob, Bill, David, Richard, Rod, Kirk, Rodney, Jerry, and Johnny) who agreed to read and participate in a review of this study during several weekly meetings. Your time and input helped me make additions and clarifications that will make the study a benefit to all who read it.

I would like to thank my woodworking friends Dave, Paul, and Mike who helped me understand the tools of the trade described in this book. Finally, I would like to express my gratitude to Terry Austin and Austin Brothers Publishing for working with me to make the release of this book possible.

Preface

Welcome to Plane Truths for Living.

Upon reading the title to this book, you might ask, "Don't you really mean Plain Truths for Living? Why did you use the word *Plane* instead of *Plain* and what is the purpose for the picture of tools on the cover? What exactly is a 'Plane' Truth?"

A Plane Truth is the revelation of a life changing truth or lesson for living, extracted through the observation of woodworkers and the use and design of a simple but age-old woodworking tool—the basic hand plane.

This book captures my journey to understand the concept of a *Plane Truth* so others might learn the importance of slowing down, spending time in quiet reflection, and gaining insight from the experience.

Can you actually gain insight about living or relating to others by observing a common tool? After all, I expect some of you have used hundreds of tools during your life without gaining any life changing truths or insights except perhaps the realization that hammers are much harder than fingers and thumbs. Others of you have had little experience with tools and picked up this book out of curiosity, or with the thought of buying it for a woodworking friend. For you, the whole subject of woodworking and hand planes probably seems foreign.

Plane Truths for Living

Human history is filled with examples of the development and use of basic tools. Some of the earliest tools consisted of stones for grinding corn, and flint arrowheads for protection or hunting. Over time, bronze and iron replaced stone,[1] but the changes did not stop there. The transition to new tools and materials has continued to take place up until today. Not only have the materials changed, but the tools themselves have become more and more sophisticated in design. Today's tablet computers and smart phones are two of the more recently developed tools. Though mostly unheard of only a few years ago, many people now consider these tools to be indispensable.

Whether you are talking about hand planes, complex computers, or the phone you use, tools quickly expand your capabilities and just as quickly become viewed as necessities. It is interesting that some tools remain useful for over hundreds of years while others have very short productive life cycles. The standard hand plane has had a comparatively long run as a useful tool. Unlike many of today's modern tools, planes are also very portable—batteries neither included nor required. Their functionality, longevity, and portability make the hand plane an attractive candidate for study.

What should you expect from this book? When finished, you should accomplish at least two things. First, you will learn more about a simple hand plane than you know today. Second, you will have an opportunity to cogitate, as my grandmother used to say, on nineteen separate lessons or truths that can be applied to your daily life. These facts, when taken to heart, have the ability to change how you live and relate to those around you.

Regardless of your knowledge of tools, consider this book a fascinating glimpse into the world of a woodworker who uses wood planes.

---
[1] Genesis 4:22

Plane Truths for Living

Along the way, you will be exposed to analogies that will relate to living your life, review related Biblical scriptures, and even get to know a few friends of mine.

Introduction

The idea for the journey into the world of woodworkers and hand planes began innocently enough with a trip to an antique tool sale. My wife might refer to these shows as flea markets, used tool sales or perhaps, on a bad day, junk sales. However, for me, none of those terms capture the sense of wonder I experienced when looking at rows of tables containing a myriad of tools used by men and women over the past 100 years.

I have recently retired after working for over thirty years as an engineer, technical writer, industry standards representative, trainer, expert witness, and planner in the telecommunications industry. Knowing that I enjoyed creative woodworking projects, my friend Dave introduced me to some of the finer points of working with wood and opened a new way for me to spend my time and the funds from my diminishing 401K.

Dave and my other woodworking friends have also expanded my understanding of the greater purpose in purchasing tools. I had always viewed tools as items to be used in the construction of a project, and in that light, they needed to make the product better or reduce the building time. I now understand some tools are purchased to set on shelves, store in drawers, gather dust, initiate discussion, and aggravate spouses.

Perhaps a woodworking friend of mine put it best when he explained the reasons for making a purchase. According to him, there are three reasons to buy any tool: 1) to use, 2) to collect and look at but not necessarily use, and 3) if you still want the tool but it does not satisfy the first two criteria, it can be purchased if it might at some point in the future be useful to you or someone else. I have noticed that the third criteria is often interpreted very loosely.

At times, it seems that a tool's functionality has little impact on its financial value. Instead, the price of an item is often dependent on how many are available and the number of individuals interested in using or collecting it. The value of some items, particularly the expensive ones, is difficult to explain to those new to the craft. As a neophyte to collecting, most of my purchases were items I thought I could use for the completion of a project while Dave's purchases tend to be driven by their worth as a collectible.

Explaining the cost versus functionality versus dust-gathering purpose of an item is often difficult to convey to the uninitiated in general, and spouses more specifically. You will also find that the difficulty in explaining the benefit of owning a particular tool is directly proportional to the price paid.

As with all collecting, having one of a particular item of a given type is rarely sufficient. This is because it is always possible to find a better or a newer, or an older version of whatever item you are collecting. You will also find that collectibles may end up being stored on shelves, in boxes, or even in showcases. Unless you keep outstanding records of your inventory, it is easy to end up purchasing a duplicate item without realizing it. Several woodworking friends and I often attend a monthly flea market to spend time visiting, looking for tools, and eating lunch together. One familiar story we often relive over lunch is the time one of us purchased a relatively expensive plow plane only to arrive home and discover he already had one exactly like it. We often joke that we would not be surprised if there is even a third identical plane in the back of a drawer or cabinet somewhere in his shop that has yet to be rediscovered. Purchasing a second or third item is surprisingly easy to do. Don't ask me how I know.

Since becoming involved in woodworking, I have developed a particular attraction for hand planes. Other woodworkers I know have a soft spot for hammers, items made from brass, or six-inch rulers. As strange as that sounds, you would be surprised how many different types of hammers and rulers there are and how expensive the really unique ones can be.

My first memory of a hand plane involved going to the hardware store with my dad to purchase a plane that he used to shave off the bottom of a door. The original door no longer fit because of carpeting we had installed. Dad's No. 5 Stanley plane now resides in my shop in a special cabinet made just for hand planes. I enjoy using it from time to time even though I also own a more expensive and technically more advanced plane of that size. Dad's plane just has a unique feel when coaxing shavings from a piece of wood. Perhaps I like planes because of the trip to the store with dad, or maybe it is just that in this world of electrically powered tools, it is nice to find something that works well without being plugged into an outlet.

With regard to planes, you soon learn there are a sufficient number of sizes, manufacturers, types, and ages to satisfy several lifetimes of collecting. Having started collecting late in life, my wife often points out that I seem to be trying to make up for lost time. In addition to attending flea markets and garage sales, you will find that most large cities have places where antique tools are displayed and sold. These venues provide an excellent opportunity to increase your collection.

Plane Truths for Living

It was during a recent visit to a local sale that I discovered a plane that changed the way I look at all tools and became the prime reason for this book. I selected the tool somewhat in haste, carrying it around for only 45 minutes before purchasing. The tool show was being held outdoors, and the weather was not cooperating. The individual that runs the show advertises that it is held rain or shine and he provides free parking, coffee, admittance, and advice.

When it comes to woodworkers shopping for a bargain you will find that like the postal service—*A little rain, sleet, or snow does not deter the avid collector from the hunt.*

I spent a considerable amount of time looking at tools on tables under tarps trying to keep from getting the tools or myself wet and not being particularly successful at either task. The plane I purchased that day was not a brand noted for its value as a collectible item or for its construction and function. In fact, I do not recall having heard of the brand prior to that Saturday. It was, I learned later, a Fulton plane, which the Sargent Tool Company produced for Sears and Roebuck between 1940 and 1964. Two things attracted me to the plane: the fact that the blade was obviously not the original and a tag the seller had taped to the side of the plane:

"Sargent #3[2] Plane, $35 'Silk Purse'."

In addition to the tag, the name Fulton and a four-digit number was stamped on one side of the plane. This plane was immediately of interest since my collection did not contain a No. 3, and the vacant spot on my shelf holding my collection of planes needed to be filled.

---

2   The numbers associated with different size planes will be explained in more detail later in the book.

Plane Truths for Living

Tool shows, flea markets, and garage sales are seldom attended with the goal of buying a particular item. Most of the time my reason for attending is driven by curiosity followed closely by the hope of finding a bargain. I have probably visited several hundred sales of one type or another, and I always seem to find something I think I need before leaving. Granted, there have been times when the total money spent was less than a dollar, or in the case of a flea market, I have purchased something completely off my radar like fresh fruits or vegetables. Since these nutritional purchases benefit the whole family, they have the added benefit of convincing my spouse of the value of my attending such events. Strange as it may seem, she is always more excited over a bag of fresh oranges or grapefruit than my purchase of a 100-year-old rusted hand plane with a chipped blade.

Regardless of the venue, I always seem to find something to discuss on the way home. Therefore, it should not surprise you that the driving factor for my attendance at this particular rainy day tool show was not caused by a desire to purchase anything in particular. We had not attended this show in over a year, and I went to review the inventory, search for items to be discussed on the way home, and renew acquaintances with the individual who ran the tool show.

Whether it was the haste necessitated by the rain, the curious note on the side of the plane, or as you may decide later, something more spiritual in nature, I purchased the plane even though it seemed a bit expensive for an unknown brand that, except for the blade, looked fairly ordinary. Once purchased, I spent a few sleepless nights trying to determine what to do with it. You see, not every investment turns out the way you would expect. In future chapters, you will follow me and my

Plane Truths for Living

struggles with a *silk purse* plane. I think you will be surprised by some of the lessons the simple hand plane can teach you.

Chapter 1
Stopping to Smell the Roses

Everyday life is a great teacher if you pay attention. Unfortunately, most of us seldom think about what we see as we go through life from day to day. When it comes to "stopping and smelling the roses," in our fast-paced world, we're fortunate even to notice there is a rose. If we do notice, we're normally hard-pressed to remember any details of what we saw. Stop and smell the roses? Do you take time for that?

Like most of us, I seem to go through my day with little notice of my surroundings. Just ask my wife if you want verification. For example, the other day, I asked her about what I thought was a new picture hanging on the wall in our kitchen only to be told it had been there for six months. You know, I really should be more careful about the questions I ask. Of course, she says I should be more observant. The good news is that after over 45 years of marriage, she has gotten somewhat used to my questions. Though accustomed to some of my mental shortcomings, she does tend to walk away mumbling something about a *guy brain*.

As I indicated earlier, my lack of observation changed briefly for me after my rainy weekend attendance at the tool show. In the days following the purchase of the *silk purse* hand plane, I experienced several revelations that caused me actually to stop and draw conclusions about what I saw. Since then, I have continued to reflect on the insight gained from the experience. Those reflections have shown me several life lessons or *Plane* Truths that should also be of help to you as you relate to the world.

Most people understand intuitively that their surroundings can cause them to think about the deeper meaning to life. The challenge is to slow down and take the time to observe and think about what we see. For example, something as simple as a wildflower growing up through a crack in the concrete can help you realize that unusual things are possible and that you, like the flower, can persevere during difficult circumstances.

When it comes to lessons for daily living, most of us expect the essential ones to appear in some earth-shattering way; "If it is critical, I will know it." While this may be true when it comes to a few of the stressful life-changing events all of us face, you will also find that it is often the simple things of life that can teach you the most. You might recall from the Old Testament (1Kings 19: 12-13), that even God's presence was not in the mighty wind or in the earthquake or in the fire. His presence was the *still small voice*.

In Psalms 37:7 we are instructed to "be still before the Lord and wait patiently for him." This instruction is not isolated to this single verse in Psalms. A word search of the Bible finds at least 14 different verses where the value of waiting on the Lord is specifically identified. If you only expect to learn from major events, you may miss some of life's subtle yet more valuable lessons. Instead of looking with anticipation for some type of explosion, spend time quietly listening for the "still small voice."

Have you noticed how soon you forget some of the lessons you learn if you don't make an effort to write them down, record them in a photograph, or perhaps discuss them from time to time? This forgetfulness often causes us to repeat the same mistakes over and over. Remember, one definition of insanity is the act of continuing to do the same thing over and over again while expecting a different outcome.[3] Growth in your physical, emotional, and spiritual life involves learning from both your successes and your failures.

God recognizes we are forgetful. He instructed the Israelites to build monuments (Joshua 4:5-7), or participate in certain religious practices and holidays, so they would not forget His action or their responsibilities. In the book of Deuteronomy, God cautions us not to forget the lessons he has taught us or what He has shown us, and even to pass those lessons learned on to our children and grandchildren:

"Only be careful and watch yourselves closely so that you do not forget the things your eyes have seen or let them slip from your heart as long as you live. Teach them to your children and to their children after them." (Deuteronomy 4:9)

It took a recent trip to a Colorado mountaintop for me to remember how magnificent the stars can be when you get away from the city lights. If I could forget this splendor, I wondered aloud at what other past miracles and blessings I had forgotten. If you have not experienced a nighttime sky in several years, it is easy to forget that the Milky Way is so much more than a candy bar. Therefore, one major reason for writing this book was to ensure I did not forget the experiences and truths that were learned from a simple hand plane. As noted in the preface, this

---

3   This quote has been attributed, perhaps incorrectly, to both Albert Einstein and Benjamin Franklin. While it actually falls short of an accurate technical definition of insanity, it does point to the problem of repeating the same mistakes.

book captures my journey in print, so that others might learn the importance of slowing down, spending some time in quiet reflection, and gaining insight from the experience.

When you consider basic hand tools—how they are made, how they function, and what they are designed to accomplish—you will find it is not a great leap to start comparing their function to your personal life, including your relationship to God and the world around you. In Romans 6:13, you and I are told to be tools or instruments of righteousness. If God, through His word, is telling us we should be a tool or instrument of righteousness, then discovering what makes an excellent hand tool may provide insight into how we can be better individuals. Not convinced yet? I don't blame you. As I mentioned earlier, the revelation received based on the comparison of tool use and life values did not occur to me immediately. In fact, I have continued to experience a greater understanding of this concept over time. As you participate in this study, I hope you will come to appreciate what it means to be a useful tool. My goal is to help you gain insight into your own life by analyzing how useful tools are designed, used, repaired, and maintained.

If you are familiar with basic woodworking tools, you may have already noticed some of the parallels between tools and individuals. If not, do not despair. Sufficient background material will be presented to help you understand the operation of a particular tool and gain an appreciation of its applications for daily living. Through a study of the analogies drawn, a review of related scripture, and time spent in thought and discussion, you should develop a deeper knowledge of what it means to be an instrument of righteousness. Perhaps it will even cause you to question how you should relate to the world at-large.

Chapter 2
Wood Planes - What Makes Them Special?

The picture below is a storage cabinet containing several planes. It provides a small-scale demonstration of the variety in size and shape of available hand planes. There are literally hundreds of different planes, each with their own unique design and purpose.

The oldest plane in existence today is from Pompeii, dating to A.D. 79.[4] It is surprising to note that it bears a striking resemblance to the planes used by 21st-century woodworkers. The basic design has made few significant changes since the days of the Roman Empire. Like those older planes, today's versions consist of a sharp blade and some device to hold the blade securely at a fixed angle. Both old and new planes allow a blade to shave off small amounts of wood as you move it over a rough wooden surface. Over the years, the materials used and some of the finer technical details in hand plane construction have certainly changed. However, if you saw a picture of the tool found in the ruins of Pompeii, you would have no trouble recognizing it as a plane.

Consider the following table and diagram to be your introduction to the world of woodworking and hand planes. While reviewing the in-

---

[4] Garrett Hack, *The Handplane Book* (The Taunton Press Inc, 1997) 15.

Plane Truths for Living

My Plane Wall Cabinet

dividual parts of a wood plane may not be the most exciting topic, this information will be critical to your understanding of the analogies in future chapters. You may even want to mark this section so that you can refer to it from time to time as you visualize the individual parts that make up a hand plane and seek to gain a better understanding of the main character in this study.

Basic Element	Description
Blade or Plane Iron[5]	A sharpened steel plate that is responsible for cutting the wood
Lever Cap	A cap with a quick release that securely holds the blade to the plane
Chip Breaker	A steel plate fastened to the top of the blade with a large screw. It provides the blade rigidity and directs the shavings away from the blade
Frog[6]	A wedge-shaped structure to which the blade, chip breaker, and lever cap are attached
Iron Base	The largest part of the plane. All other parts attach to this base.
Mouth or Throat	The slot in the iron base the blade goes through to contact the wood
Tote	The handle at the back of the plane
Depth Adjustment Wheel	A wheel at the back of the frog designed to gradually advance or retract the blade, depending on the direction turned
Lateral Adjustment Wheel	A leaver at the back of the frog used to move the blade from side to side to insure the cutting edge is parallel to the bottom of the plane
Sole	The bottom of the iron base of the plane that presents a flat surface to the wood being planed

While there will be differences in manufacturer and size, basic hand planes contain most, if not all, the parts shown in the diagram on the next page. The quality, detailed design, and cost will, of course, vary. The plane pictured in the exploded view below is a No. 3 plane and is

---

[5] You will find both "Blade" and "Plane Iron" in the literature. However, the term blade will be used in this study for simplicity.

[6] The origin of the name "Frog" is unclear. Some think it is because the structure resembles a frog, and others claim it was used due to the devices' proximity to the throat of the plane and the old saying "do you have a frog in your throat."

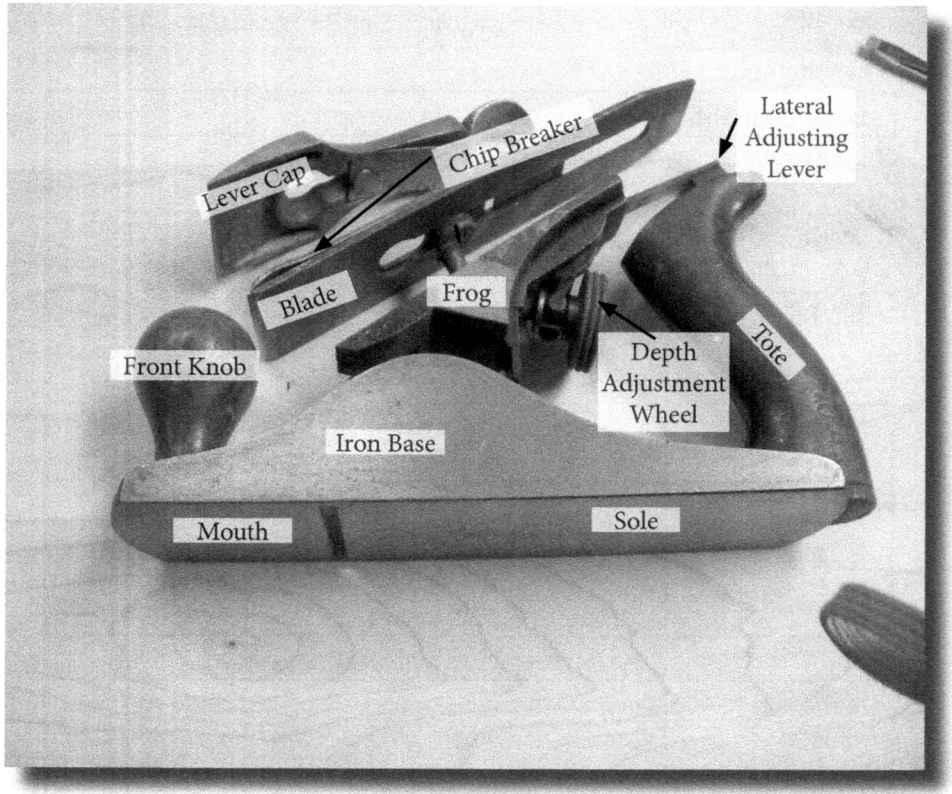

Expanded View of a Smoothing Plane

similar, but not identical to the *silk purse* plane I purchased at the tool show.

As we go through the study, the function of these parts will be discussed in greater detail. For now, simply understand that the No. 3 plane is the smallest of a group of planes called smoothing planes, and it is a little over 9" in length and 2" in width. Its intended purpose is to smooth the surface of a piece of lumber or incrementally reduce the size of a piece of wood.

One example of its use would be to plane the sides of a tight newly constructed cabinet drawer that simply needs to have a few thousandths of an inch of wood removed to make it slide in and out freely. Its width makes it an excellent choice to plane the edge of a ¾" board without tipping from side to side. Another use is to correct mistakes in construction by allowing you to reshape your project gradually. It can also be used for what its name implies, smoothing rough wood. Using a plane for this purpose is quieter than a dust-producing power sander and often produces a smoother surface.

With the possible exception of cedar fencing, wood at the neighborhood hardware store has already had all four sides smoothed prior to shipping. The construction of fine hardwood furniture often requires wood of different types and thicknesses not typically available at the local lumber yard. Woodworkers often obtain material for the projects from stores specializing in hardwood, and the wood comes to them from a lumber mill in *rough-cut* form. The term *rough-cut* implies the lumber still has the circular marks made by the saw that cut the tree into planks. You can pay the store to run the lumber through their electric planer, but where is the fun in that?[7] Smoothing the lumber yourself also gives you more control over thickness of the wood and, I think, makes for a better final product.

Once the lumber is inside your shop, you can create a smooth surface by running it through your own dusty, noisy, electric planer or you can smooth it using handheld planes. The decision on whether to use a hand plane or electric planer often comes down to the size of the project, the time available, and of course, whether you own an electric planer. If it is a major project with a lot of lumber, you might want to use

---

7   Electric planer - sometimes referred to as a thickness planer, utilizes cutting blades equally spaced around a motor driven cylinder to plane boards to a desired thickness. Raising or lowering the cutting cylinder determines the thickness of the output. Those used by woodworkers can accommodate boards approximately 12 inches wide and several inches thick. They are usually mounted to a bench or portable cart and require a vacuum attachment. The noise level for these devices sometimes exceeds 100 decibels so using them requires ear protection.

an electric planer. However, even large projects can benefit from the use of hand planes during some phase of construction.

Early in the last century, plane manufacturers developed a naming convention using a series of numbers to identify different types of planes.[8] This naming convention has been used for the past 100 years and greatly simplifies the comparison of planes regardless of manufacturer. Therefore a No. 3 plane sold by any of a number of different companies has essentially the same shape, size, and angle with which the blade contacts the wood. That does not mean that all No. 3 planes are identical. Though the basic design is similar, there are often vast difference between each company's planes regarding the quality of the materials used in construction, the fit of the individual parts, and the ease of use. There may even be quality differences between models of tools made by the same manufacturer.

Now that you have a basic understanding of the component parts of a hand plane and know a little of the story that started me on the road to writing this book, it is time to learn some *Plane Truths*. The next chapter will serve as a reminder that life does not always provide you and those you know with a smooth path to travel. What should be your response when you or your acquaintances experience a rough spot in daily life?

---

[8] This naming convention has grown to identify approximately 200 different plane types that vary in design shape and purpose.

Chapter 3
And The Rough Places Plain

In addition to making wood smooth to the touch, some planes, such as the 22-inch-long No. 7 jointer plane, are designed for creating very flat boards. The term *flat* is of course relative. I grew up in Lubbock, Texas, known for its lack of geographic variability. The difference between the highest and lowest point in this city with a population of approximately 250,000 is only 150 feet, and most newcomers consider that very flat. After discussing this concept with a friend from Florida, I have come to realize that Lubbock is mountainous when compared to some areas of Florida.

To a carpenter building a house, differences of a quarter of an inch or more are often considered acceptable. However, if you operate a machine shop, the degree of flatness may be measured in thousands of an inch. With regard to woodworking and furniture construction, an error of several hundredths of an inch may sometimes be noticeable. Therefore, you will never hear a woodworker complain that the component parts of a project are too flat or too straight.

I was first introduced to the need for straight flat boards in high school Shop Class. For our initial project, we were issued a hand plane and a slightly misshapen block of wood. Remember Shop Class? That was where the boys went while the girls were in Home Economics learning to cook and sew. It was also the place where, as Bill Cosby liked to point out, you could always take a failed project, "cut two grooves in it and call it an ashtray."[9] My how things have changed! It is great that we now have more ladies involved in woodworking and guys involved in cooking. It is also great that most do not have a need for an ashtray.

Our assignment was to remove the least amount of wood from the block while at the same time ensuring all adjacent surfaces were at 90 degrees to each other. The project sounded simple at first. Then I realized that a cube has six flat sides, eight pointed corners, and twenty-four right angles. I spent a long time completing the project. As I attempted to plane off just enough wood to square the block, some efforts actually made things worse. The final product ended up being a block of wood that was far smaller than what I started with. I remember being grateful that the shop teacher took pity on me and gave me a passing grade on the project. When the shop teacher assigned the wooden block project, he told us that creating flat, square surfaces was a basic woodworking skill. Without this ability, he said, we would have difficulty successfully completing all future projects.

One of the more demanding requirements for flat straight boards occurs when you are constructing items with broad surfaces such as the top of a table or cabinet. While you can sometimes obtain boards in widths exceeding 12 inches, you frequently find yourself using widths of 5 to 8 inches. Therefore, smaller boards must generally be joined together side by side to obtain the desired width. For example, if you need a top ¾ of an inch thick, twelve inches wide and four feet long, you can join two boards that are six inches wide, ¾ thick and four feet long. If the ¾ inch edges of the two boards being joined are not very flat over

---

9   Bill Cosby comedy album "Why is There Air."

the total 4 feet length when laid side by side, gaps will appear between them as they are glued together.

In addition to the aesthetic problems these gaps create, the joint between the two boards will be weak. This is because you will essentially be trying to glue air in the sections where the gaps occur. Any gaps that are not eliminated prior to gluing the wood will need to be filled with wood putty for esthetic reasons prior to finishing. But if the joints have gaps, the bond between the two narrow boards will not be strong, and the boards may even break apart at some point. I have found that if a failure occurs, it usually happens late in the construction process making it difficult to correct.

The edges of boards can be flattened using a power jointer, a table saw with a long straight fence or a No. 7 jointer plane. The No. 7 plane's length makes it ideal for flattening the edges of both boards to be glued together. This is because it allows you to create a mirror image of the bottom of the plane over the entire board by lowering any high spots.

Number 7 vs. Number 3

Shorter planes such as the #3 will not flatten long boards since they merely follow the contour of the board making it smooth but not necessarily flat. Once the boards are flattened, you should be able to lay them side by side and their edges should touch along the entire length with no gaps. If the board's edges are flat and you select wood with similar grain pattern, the seam between the different boards may be nearly invisible once they have been glued together and varnished. The picture above shows the difference in size between a No. 3 Smoothing Plane shown earlier and the much larger No. 7.

While thinking of the requirement for flat straight surfaces, I was reminded of the chorus from Handle's Messiah, *Every Valley Shall be Exalted*. This chorus is taken from the book of Isaiah.

"Every valley shall be exalted, and every mountain and hill shall be made low: and the crooked shall be made straight, and the rough places plain." (Isaiah 40:4 KJV)

This verse was chosen for the cover as it describes the function of a hand plane. If you have not heard the chorus in a while, search for it on the Internet and see if you do not agree with me. With regard to wood, a plane raises the valleys by making the mountains low. It also makes the crooked straight and the rough places like a flat plain.

From a Biblical perspective, you are also called to make rough places like a flat plain in your personal life. Just like the surface of two boards being joined together, presenting smooth surfaces to others makes your working relationship much more enjoyable. Unfortunately, far too many individuals do just the opposite. They often seem to present their rough edges, and in response to life's situations, make smooth places rough and rough places even worse or more uncomfortable for themselves and others.

Like an improperly adjusted hand plane or one with a dull blade, those who present their rough edges to the world end up creating more problems than they solve. To a woodworker, nothing is worse than attempting to make that one final smoothing pass on a piece of wood only to find that because of problems with the plane, there is now a deep groove where smooth wood should have been. To resolve the problem, the plane will need to be readjusted, perhaps the blade sharpened, and the whole surface of the project reworked. Whether you are talking about hand planes or individuals, the guidance of the Master is necessary to finish projects without creating rough places properly.

Plane Truth #1: You are called to be a tool in the hands of the Master and as such make rough places smooth.

Scriptures #1

"Blessed are the peacemakers, for they will be called the sons of God." (Matthew 5:9)

"Be still before the Lord and wait patiently for him; do not fret when men succeed in their ways, when they carry out their wicked schemes. Refrain from anger and turn from wrath; do not fret—it leads only to evil. For evil men will be cut off, but those who hope in the Lord will inherit the land." (Psalms 37:7-9)

"A gentle answer turns away wrath, but a harsh word stirs up anger." (Proverbs 15:1)

"Peacemakers who sow in peace raise a harvest of righteousness." (James 3:18)

"Make every effort to live in peace with all men and to be holy; without holiness no one will see the Lord." (Hebrews 12:14)

"For we are God's workmanship, created in Christ Jesus to do good works, which God prepared in advance for us to do." (Ephesians 2:10)

Note: Remember what Paul told Timothy in 2 Timothy 3:16 – "All Scripture is God-breathed and is useful for teaching, rebuking, correcting and training in righteousness." Each future chapter will contain a section with scripture that relates to a *Plane Truth*. At the end of each chapter, reread the verses and reflect on how they relate to the associated *Plane Truth*.

Application #1

The scriptures above should provide guidance as you strive to make the rough places in your life and the lives of others smooth. Do you want to be blessed? Jesus states, in the first scripture reference above, that peacemakers will be blessed. In the five additional references, you are instructed to refrain from anger, be gentle in your conversation, sow in peace, live in peace, and finally, Paul points out that you are created to do the works God has prepared for you. God has not prepared you for evil works! Reread these verses again and consider them God's guidelines.

If you have difficulty being a peacemaker, start by seeking out and supporting those who are gentle in spirit and are known for their ability to smooth out the rough spots in the lives of others. Observe how they handle stressful situations. You can tell a lot about an individual from this observation. Do they make excuses, rant, and rave, or perhaps blame others for their current situation? Or do they more calmly analyze the situation, let go of the past, and move forward to a resolution?

I observed different responses to stress from two individuals during a business trip to Tampa, Florida several years ago. A group of us had spent several days there and were headed to the airport to fly back home. On the way to the Tampa airport, we were discussing what had transpired the past few days and missed our exit. While a missed turn is usually not a big problem, this error placed us on the causeway headed to Clearwater.

This causeway was an elevated roadway over the water with no option to turn around for approximately 10 miles. This would have been bad enough, but we were running late, and this mistake could very well mean that we would all miss our flights. We had no one to blame but ourselves, but one of the individuals in our group began to rant and rave about how poor the signage on the highway was concerning the exit. He went on and on blaming the city of Tampa, the Florida Department of Transportation, and anyone else he could think of for our unfortunate situation. It was interesting to note that he did not blame himself or the rest of us for our lack of attention. While this was going on, the driver tried to calm everyone down by identifying the time remaining before the flight left and the estimated distance we now needed to travel. In the end, we were able to return the rental car and clear security just in time to make our flight. However, I will never forget one individual's unpleasant grumbling in response to a stressful situation.

It is easy to remain calm when the sea is flat, and nothing is rocking your boat. However, let a storm come up, and you'll quickly be able to tell who is in control. In addition to an inner peace and self-control, peacekeepers truly have a love for others. If you have difficulty loving the unlovable with whom you come in contact, read and spend time thinking about the message found in chapter 13 of the New Testament book of 1st Corinthians.

Are you making the rough places smooth in your world? Don't forget you are called to be a peacemaker. Do your neighbors and friends see you as a peacemaker? When I was in the military, I knew an individual who would often come into the break room and start a conversation. Whatever the topic, he always seemed to take a position guaranteed to produce an argument among those in the room. When the debate was underway, and opposing sides had been taken by groups within the room, he would disappear satisfied that he had created chaos. We need to be the ones who throw water on the fires that erupt between individuals and groups, not gasoline. This thought brings us to Plane Truth #2

Plane Truth #2: Rough places also occur between fellow Christians and within churches. God's word gives you special guidance in how to handle these rough spots in interpersonal relations.

Scriptures #2

Conflicts between Christians have occurred since Jesus' time. Paul addresses the need to keep Christian interactions smooth in several of his letters to early churches.

"I appeal to you brothers, in the name of our Lord Jesus Christ, that all of you agree with one another so that there may be no divisions among you and that you may be perfectly united in mind and thought." (1 Corinthians 1:10)

"You are still worldly. For since there is jealousy and quarreling among you, are you not worldly? Are you not acting like mere men?" (1 Corinthians 3:3)

"The acts of the sinful nature are obvious: sexual immorality, impurity and debauchery; idolatry and witchcraft; hatred, discord, jealousy, fits of rage, selfish ambition, dissensions, factions and envy; drunkenness, orgies, and the like. I warn you, as I did before, that those who live like this will not inherit the kingdom of God." (Galatians 5:19-21)

"As a prisoner for the Lord, then, I urge you to live a life worthy of the calling you have received. Be completely humble and gentle; be patient, bearing with one another in love. Make every effort to keep the unity of the Spirit through the bond of peace." (Ephesians 4:1-3)

"Have nothing to do with foolish and stupid arguments, because you know they produce quarrels. And the Lord's servant must not quarrel; instead, he must be kind to everyone, able to teach, not resentful." (2 Timothy 2:23-24)

Application #2

Just in case you think that interpersonal problems are only limited to your regular work day or to interactions with non-Christians, a quick read of the verses listed above should convince you that problems may exist even within a church setting. The following story describes a meeting at a church my family once attended. The contentious *rough spot* discussion occurred during a quarterly church business meeting. Since that day, I have often reflected back on the experience and have come to realize that if there is stress within a church, it is very likely to manifest itself during a business meeting.

In this church, as has been the case in a number of those we have attended, regularly scheduled business meetings were held, usually on Sunday night, for the purpose of discussing more worldly items that impacted the normal function of the church. These meetings provided an opportunity to review the current financial status of the church, approve the annual budget, vote on individuals nominated to serve on various committees, and provide a forum to address issues impacting the general function of the church.

Even if you have not participated in church business meetings, I suspect you recognize problems often occur in secular meetings as well. For example, have you ever experienced a contentious school board, city council, or state and federal legislative meeting? I am not sure why individuals seem to leave their good manners and good behavior at the door before attending these meetings, but it often appears to be the case. You would hope that meetings of religious groups would be immune from these problems, but my experience leads me to believe that is often not the case.

During this meeting, the difficulty concerned whether to use paper plates and plastic utensils or china and flatware at the monthly church potluck dinner. The church had sufficient plates and flatware to accommodate the number of individuals who generally attended so you would think this would be a simple problem to resolve. Far from it!

The two sides of the issue seemed to break down into 1) the economists who pointed out that "God wanted us to be good stewards"—using the plates and flatware on hand would save the church money since we would not need to purchase paper products, and 2) those who felt the time required to clean and store the dishes could be better spent in fellowship. They even quoted the story of Mary and Martha from Luke 10:38-42 as justification for this position. In this passage, Martha was upset because her sister Mary was spending time listening to Jesus rather than assisting her with the preparation of the meal. Jesus tells Martha not to be troubled and points out that Mary was right to spend time in fellowship.

It did not help matters that a significant percentage of those arguing for fellowship were the women of the church who usually washed the dishes, and the economists were overwhelmingly made up of the men in the church who normally visited while the dishes were washed. As I recall, this discussion went on for over two hours and got quite heated at times. There were a few peacemakers in the congregation who attempted to find some middle ground. They finally resolved the issue by asking for volunteers (men and women) from the congregation who would be willing to wash the dishes. Although peace was made, no one could categorize this two-hour discussion as Christian fellowship.

You may notice that well-meaning, sincere individuals can often quote scripture to back up their position. However, as you see from this example, the simple act of quoting Scripture does not necessarily make your position correct or create godly fellowship. I have also learned that this argument was not isolated to this one small church. A friend described an almost identical business meeting he had attended where the issue involved the change from glass communion glasses to plastic ones.

The scriptures listed above should help you recognize that arguments within churches are not unique to our modern age. The first two scripture verses above are from the book of 1 Corinthians and are but a sample of what Paul had to say concerning the rough spots this church was experiencing. Paul had heard that there were arguments among its members, and he knew how damaging that could be to the mission Christ had called them to perform.

The scripture from the fifth chapter of the book of Galatians provides an extensive list of actions that are called "acts of the sinful nature" or works that do not honor God. Are you surprised to read that hatred, discord, jealousy, fits of rage, selfish ambition, dissensions, factions, and envy make this list? You should also read Galatians 5:22-26 where the "fruit of the Spirit" is explained. In verse 26, Paul reminds us not to become conceited, or provoke one another. In Ephesians 4:1-3 Paul says you are to bear with one another in love. To put it in today's language, Paul is telling you to put up with one another in love. The last scripture verse listed, 2 Timothy seems to speak directly to the church argument that occurred concerning dishes. Do you think reading it to the congregation would have shortened the meeting?

Remember back to a time when you were driving on a stretch of bad highway and then suddenly come to a smooth section that had been recently paved. Not only is the noise level and vibration reduced, but the smooth road turns what had been a white-knuckle ride into an enjoyable experience. Plane Truth #1 and #2 should remind you that God calls you to make the rough places smooth regardless of where they occur. If you do, life will be more enjoyable for everyone concerned.

Chapter 3 Questions

1. Can you think of an example where a well-meaning individual from the Bible failed to heed Christ's call to be a peacemaker? Think of an example of someone you have known during your lifetime that understood Christ's directive concerning peacemakers but failed to obey. Why do you think they failed?

2. What can you do during the next seven days to make life smooth for someone else?

3. How often do you allow others to control your actions and response to situations?

4. Think of at least three individuals you consider to have been peacemakers. What did they do that makes you view them in this light? In selecting the three people choose someone you have known personally, someone from the Bible, and someone who has lived during the past 100 years.

5. The Bible has a number of verses concerning the requirement for fellow Christians to live in peace with each other. Why do you think Paul spends so much time addressing it in his letters? Does the scripture in James 4:1 provide any help in answering this question?

6. What was the problem in 1 Corinthians 11 that distressed Paul and was one of the reasons he wrote a letter to the church? Can you think of similar problems from today's world?

Chapter 4
Being Content

A wide variety of woodworking tools are available for purchase. They vary in size, shape, quality, age, and price. While you can purchase a simple table saw for as little as $100 to $200, my friend Dave indicated that no serious woodworker should be satisfied with one unless the value was in the $1,000 to $1,500 range. He communicated this fact not by specific words but with his non-verbal response to my plan to start my shop with the purchase of a saw made by a manufacturer known to provide lower cost tools.

One thing you will realize as you enter into the hobby or craft of woodworking is that your tool budget will be quickly exhausted. Unless you are independently wealthy, purchasing tools for your shop will be a continual balancing act between functionality and price. Therefore, your happiness should not depend on the cost, quality, or quantity of your tools. This battle will be a never ending one since newer and more expensive additional or replacement tools will always be available. You may have noticed that this situation is true not only for woodworking but for most other hobbies or activities. There will always be more things available to buy than the existing budget will allow. Just ask any golfer, sailor, fisherman, RV owner, hunter—well you get the idea.

Why do you think we are so easily convinced that the newer model will make us a better craftsman, fisherman, or golfer? Perhaps it is because we are all looking for the easy way out, and can always identify weakness in the equipment we already own. When you think about your older tools, consider that they were all new at one time and were initially purchased because someone thought they would make their life easier.

I recently experienced a woodworking problem that reminded me of a passage from the Old Testament, often referred to as the story of the widow and the oil (2 Kings 4:1-7). In this story, a widow had been left destitute and in debt after the death of her husband. The bill collectors had come to her house and threatened to force her two young sons into slavery to pay the families' debts. When she went to the prophet Elisha for help, one of the first things he asked her was what did she have in her house. Her response was that she had nothing, and then, almost an afterthought, she adds "except a jar of oil." God blessed the oil she had and allowed it to multiply to fill many jars. She sold the oil, and with the money she made was able to pay off her debts and live on what was left over.

The prophet's question and her initial response should provide you guidance when you are considering the purchase of that next shiny new tool. When faced with a problem, do you ever ask yourself if it could be solved using something you already own? If you are like me, I suspect that far too often you think it is necessary to purchase some new device that a TV spokesperson or magazine advertisement assures you will not only solve your problem but also bring you happiness. The next time you face a challenge, I encourage you to analyze what you already have available carefully. Answer the prophet's question, "What do you have in your house?"

I was reminded of this principle when trying to finish the top of a newly constructed chest. The wood had some interesting grain patterns and was proving difficult to plane with my smoothing plane. I had read that a type of plane called a scraper plane should be used for this type of wood. I even found a beautiful new scraper plane on the Internet for just over $200 and was thinking about purchasing it when I received a woodworking magazine with an article on the Stanley No. 80 cabinet scraper plane. Seeing this article reminded me that several years ago I had purchased a used Stanley No. 80 at a flea market for $10.

A No. 80 plane is a relatively simple device that has been manufactured for over 80 years and uses a blade mounted at a high angle to the surface of the wood. As its name implies, it removes wood with a scraping motion instead of the cutting action of the previously discussed smoothing plane. My earlier attempts to use this No. 80 plane had resulted in less than satisfactory results. Therefore, I had not even considered it an option for finishing my new chest.

I know what you are thinking. I had read that I needed a scraper plane. I had an older plane that was called a scraper plane. So, why wasn't the plane I already owned my first choice? My only excuse is that a shiny new tool seemed more desirable than the older plane that had failed to perform successfully in the past.

After reading the magazine article, it became apparent that most of the previous problems I had experienced with the scraper were the result of operator error. Given the simple design of the plane, I am still a little embarrassed to admit my shortcoming in this area. Have you ever noticed that even simple things can appear difficult if you lack information? In this case, I had lacked the knowledge to sharpen and align the blade properly. I had thought I knew what I was doing, and when things did not work out, it seemed easier to blame the tool and buy a new expensive replacement.

Armed with the new information from the magazine article, I began a search of my shop for the old plane. "Now where did I put that?" Luckily, my shop is small and the plane fairly large, so I was able to locate it without too much difficulty. Once the blade was properly sharpened and positioned, I found it to be an excellent choice for addressing my woodworking problem. It certainly turned out to be a more economical option than purchasing a new plane. The moral to the story: 1) there is power in knowledge and 2) you should look at what you have before buying something new. I also learned that you do not need another new tool to be effective or content.

No. 80 Cabinet Scraper Plane

Plane Truth #3: If you are looking for contentment based on what you own, or would like to own, you will be unhappy a lot of the time. Strive to follow Paul's example concerning contentment as described in Philippians 4:11-13.

Scripture #3

"I have learned to be content whatever the circumstances. I know what it is to be in need, and I know what it is to have plenty. I have learned the secret of being content in any and every situation, whether well fed or hungry, whether living in plenty or in want. I can do everything through him who gives me strength." (Philippians 4:11-13)

Application #3

Contrary to what the world would like you to believe, contentment does not come from having an increasing number of possessions. The world is filled with examples of wealthy and famous individuals who have accumulated a considerable number of *toys* but lead very troubled and unhappy lives. It also seems that all too often these individuals' lives end in tragedy. Paul attests to the fact that you can learn to be content whatever your situation.

Someone will always offer a more expensive item with new features to tempt you. However, most woodworkers learn that not everyone can afford or needs a $3,000 table saw or a $1,000 hand plane. Besides, if you focus on what you don't have instead of using what you do have, you will create less and be less content with life as a whole. This concept, of course, extends to other areas in life outside of your hobbies.

My dad always spoke of wanting an Oyster Rolex watch. I often wondered why the lack of that particular watch seemed to bother him since he did not desire other expensive items. He led what many would consider a frugal lifestyle, only buying used cars and even retreaded tires. He was in his 80s before he had a credit card, and to my knowledge never owned a watch that cost over $100. A discussion with his older brother gave me a window into why he had this desire. Dad wanted it not because he needed to keep track of time but because his father, my grandfather, had bought one for my dad's brother at the Army PX in the 1940s.

My grandfather was going to purchase one for my father as well, but dad was overseas at the time. His father became ill and passed away before my dad returned to the states, and he never got the watch his father wanted to buy him. By the time dad tried to purchase one at the PX, they were no longer available. It is a testament to his character that while he talked of buying one for over 40 years, he preferred to spend his money on other things, like raising his family, making it possible for me and my brother to attend college—debt free, and doing proper estate planning that ensured my mother was well cared for after his death. Dad could distinguish the difference between a genuine need and a want.

Have you noticed that whether you are talking about watches, golf clubs, or woodworking tools, the price and quality of items can vary widely? Each new release of a product will also claim to offer features not available on older models. Continuing to wish for the newest most feature-rich item can be a costly, frustrating process and will not produce long term contentment. Remember, spending a lot of time wishing for what you don't have reduces the time you have to use what you *do* have to make something useful.

While most of you would agree that having adversity in your life makes it difficult to be content, if you are honest, you would also agree that dealing with abundance can also brings challenges that can have a negative impact. Paul states in Philippians 4 that his faith gave him the strength to be content regardless of what he did or did not have. He also indicates that he had not always been able to be content in all situations. He says he had "learned" to be content implying that at some point in the past this was not so.

Remember, the possessions you own can be lost or taken away. The situations you face from day to day will not always go your way. True contentment must be based on something longer lasting than life's day to day experiences or what you own.

Chapter 4 Questions

1. Is some material possession you currently desire keeping you from being content? How can you keep your desires for possessions in their proper perspective?

2. Read Hebrews 13:5. Does this verse provide any additional insight concerning your answer to question 1?

3. How do you think Paul was able to learn "to be content" in whatever situation he found himself? Read 2 Corinthians 11:24-27. List the reasons Paul had not to be content.

4. Give some examples of "famous" individuals considered successful but unhappy during their lifetime. Why were they unhappy?

5. Do you know someone you would consider truly happy? What do you think is the secret of their happiness? How do possessions impact their happiness?

Chapter 5
Life Is Temporary

In the last chapter, you were introduced to the concept of contentment. You learned that many people think that accumulating money and things will make them content. However, basing your state of mind on what you own will typically ensure you are never satisfied. In this chapter, you will learn that purchasing a new item you thought you needed not only does not bring contentment, but the product itself may quickly become obsolete. The product life cycle of many of today's purchases can be relatively short. One advantage of buying a good used hand plane is that the price does not normally break your tool budget and their useful life may be longer than yours.

Other than marveling at tools of the past, another purpose for attending a tool show is to determine an antique tool's intended purpose or function. The original use of some of the older tools displayed at a tool show sometimes escapes even the knowledge of the individual selling them. In response to the question "What was that used for?" you may often hear, "I brought it here in hopes someone could tell me." The sense of wonder and the engineer in me enjoys the search and the discussion that ensues when a particularly strange looking device is found.

For example, we came upon an interesting tool at the flea market the other day. It had a cone-shaped piece of metal mounted on the lower part of an L-shaped iron bracket. Above the cone was mounted a round wooden cylinder about 10 inches long and 4 inches in diameter that rotated. It looked like some type of farm implement, but neither Dave nor I could guess its intended purpose. This time the seller did know what it was. It was a special plow developed in 1910 for harvesting sweet potatoes. While I guess someone could consider this a useful item, we decided our collections did not need it at this particular time.

The obvious additional purpose in attending a tool show is to purchase something interesting that can be used in the shop. Over the past few years, Dave and I have visited flea markets, swap meets, garage sales, estate sales, and tool shows in search of that ever-elusive interesting tool that is priced just right. It might be purchased to use immediately, or it may find its place on a shelf in the shop to gather dust and await the call to solve some yet unknown requirement. At the very least these tools give us something to discuss as we drive to the next tool show.

It may be that these new purchases added to our collection, when opportunities present themselves, will allow our family at some point, hopefully far in the future, to question our sanity, laugh about "why dad bought this" and try to determine how to dispose of our precious items at the inevitable estate sale. After purchasing a particularly expensive tool, we often joke that our children will probably sell it at some point in the future for $5 or less.

Many of the tools we see at shows have long since outlived their usefulness, making their function difficult to determine. One example some of you may recall is the device that was used to open a can of motor oil. You remember a motor oil can, don't you? Oil for your car engine has not always been available in a plastic bottle with a screw-off cap. It once came in a one-quart metal can and required a special device that combined the function of opening a hole in the lid while at the same time providing a spout for pouring the oil into the engine. Sure, you could have used a standard can opener instead of this specialized device, but pouring would not have been as easy.

You remember a can opener, don't you? It was developed back in the 1930s to open liquid filled cans and pop the tops off bottles. I am not referring to the electric device you may have in your kitchen today that removes the top of a can, although new can designs with pull tabs to remove the tops may soon make these obsolete as well. This older device had a point on one end and allowed you to punch a small triangular shaped hole at the top edge of the can. The other end had a curved shaped used to pop the caps off bottles. Remember when bottle caps had to be pried instead of twisted off. If you still don't know what I am referring to, look up the term "church key" on the Internet. While a church key could be used to open an oil can, the modification that combined the spout with the opener was a significant advancement in its day and made the job of changing your car's oil much simpler and cleaner. The motor oil can opener became obsolete between 1980 and 1990, shortly after they stopped selling motor oil in cans. You can occasionally find one of these openers at flea markets and garage sales but ask for one at your local auto parts store and see what they tell you. Below you will find a picture of these two types of can openers from the past.

Have you ever thought about what causes a device to become obsolete? Why do some items far outlive their original owners and

Oil Can Openers from the Past

continue to be used and useful after over 100 years, while others are discarded as worthless in a relatively short period of time? Just like the tools being discussed, you and I have a limited time for being effective. Only God knows what that time frame will be. Whether it is a tool or an individual, all things are temporary.

Plane Truth #4: Recognize that the Lord has given you today and you should use it for His glory. You have no guarantee of what will happen tomorrow.

Scriptures #4

"As for man, his days are as grass, he flourishes like a flower of the field; the wind blows over it and it is gone, and its place remembers it no more." (Psalms 103:15-16)

"Why, you do not even know what will happen tomorrow. What is your life? You are a mist that appears for a little while and then vanishes." (James 4:14)

"Who of you by worrying can add a single hour to your life?" (Luke 12:25)

Application #4

The first two verses remind us that life is short and even the most famous among us may not be remembered long after they leave this earth. It is interesting that when the newspaper lists birthdays of famous individuals, there are fewer and fewer names I recognize. My children, on the other hand, know everyone except for the ones I can identify. When I attend an estate sale, I often wonder if the previous owners are still alive and if they realized as the second verse above says, "you do not even know what will happen tomorrow."

Estate sales provide an interesting look into the lives of others in that they often reveal what the owners thought were important. Items believed to be precious by their former owner often end up being sold for little or nothing, given to charity, or in some cases becoming additions to the nearest landfill. This should remind you that everything you may now consider a cherished possession will one day be of no value to you, or others.

This concept was brought home to me as I experienced an interesting change in my mom's perspective that occurred after my dad passed away. Shortly after the funeral, my brother and I and our spouses were attempting to help mom organize some of the things in dad's closet. Her response to us was "please do not touch my stuff." Over a year later when she had decided to sell the house and move into a one-bedroom apartment in an assisted living facility, we were trying to help her determine what to do with some of the things in the house. She had decided to have a garage sale and in preparation for the sale asked us to bring her things to her as she sat in a chair and told us what to do with them. Some of the very same things that a year before had elicited the response "don't touch my stuff" now received the response, "get rid of it, it is just stuff".

At some point, many of the items we now view as precious will become *just stuff*. To paraphrase the old gospel song, "This world is not our home, we're just a passin' through."[10] Regardless of your age, no one is promised tomorrow. As the verse from Luke 12:25 above points out, we cannot add a day to our life by worrying about it. In fact, modern science tells us that worrying about things may actually shorten our lives.

You may think you have many years ahead, and hopefully, you do. I once heard a preacher say that if you are thirty years of age but are only going to live another five years, you are old. On the other hand, if you are fifty and will live another forty years you are still young. Only God knows whether you are young or old.

Do you live as if you have plenty of time to accomplish your dreams and future plans? How long is your bucket list of things you intend to do tomorrow? If you want your legacy to be something more than "he or she worked their whole life, and then they died," now is the time to change. This does not mean you should not plan for tomorrow. The Bible has a number of verses explaining the benefit of making wise long-term financial and personal decisions. However, you should recognize that some things should not be put off until tomorrow. Remember, tomorrow may never come.

I suspect your most often delayed actions are the things you intend to do for or with family members and friends. Since friends and family also have a limited time on earth, delays in this area can result

---
10   Albert E Brumley, This world is not my home, 1937.

in some of the greatest long-term disappointments of life. One of my friends liked to demonstrate this principle as it relates to children by stating "you can't take an 18-year-old to the circus." When considering those important things that continually end up on your *do tomorrow list*, ask yourself: if I do not do it today when exactly will I do it?

Chapter 5 Questions

1. What items might you see at an estate sale that at one time had value to an individual, but now has little value to others? What limits its value?

2. What things, in your life today, do you place more value on than you should?

3. If you found out that you had only one year to live, what would be on your bucket list? Would the recognition of this reduced lifespan change how you spent your time? If so, what changes would you make and how soon? If you would make no changes, why would that be the case?

4. Why do you think some people seem to be efficient and productive into their eighties and nineties while others appear to withdraw from society when they are much younger? What keeps those in your age group from being effective and productive?

5. How large is your sphere of influence today? What could you change to increase the number of people your life positively impacts?

Chapter 6
What Does Age Have to Do with It?

As you discovered in the last chapter, some lives on earth may be shorter than others, and none of us is guaranteed how many years we have left. You should strive to make an impact during the time you are here regardless of your current age. This chapter explores what the age of a hand plane or an individual has to do with their ability to serve and be of service.

In today's world, you are often told that the new model is always better. In the world of hand tools, this is not always the case. A few select manufacturers do make new excellent and expensive hand planes. There are also some new planes you can purchase today that are much less functional and productive than those planes of the past. The longer you are around hand tools, the more you realize the age is not an indicator of quality. There are excellent old tools and poor quality old tools just as there are excellent new tools and poor quality new tools You will also find that the mere fact that something is old does not make it collectible or a joy to use.

Would it surprise you to know there are excellent 100-year-old planes still available today? These planes were built to last, and with a little cleanup work can often be restored to their original capability. In fact, with the addition of a modern high-quality blade, they may be even better than when they were new. *Stanley's Bedrock* planes, manufactured in the early part of the 20th century, are a good example. They are great planes, easy to use, and still routinely sell on the Internet for over $100. At the same time, some newer versions of planes made by well-known manufacturers do not always have the functionality or value of older planes and sell used for $10 to $20. The truth is, you just can't determine a plane's value or how well it will function based on its age alone. Just because a tool is shiny does not necessarily mean it will be effective.

Plane Truth #5: As with hand planes, when it comes to your ability to serve and be of service, age is not a factor to consider.

Scriptures #5

"This applies to the Levites: Men twenty-five years old or more shall come to take part in the work of the Tent of Meeting, but at the age of fifty, they must retire from their regular service and work no longer. They may assist their brothers in performing their duties at the Tent of Meetings, but they themselves must not do the work." (Numbers 8: 24-26)

"Therefore, since we are surrounded by such a great cloud of witnesses, let us throw off everything that hinders and the sin that so easily entangles, and let us run with perseverance the race marked out for us." (Hebrews 12:1)

"The righteous will flourish like a palm tree, they will grow like a cedar of Lebanon; planted in the house of the Lord, they will flourish in the courts of our God. They will still bear fruit in old age, they will stay fresh and green, proclaiming, "The Lord is upright; he is my Rock, and there is no wickedness in him." (Psalms 92:12-15)

"Don't let anyone look down on you because you are young, but set an example for the believers in speech, in life, in love, in faith and in purity." (1 Timothy 4:12)

Application #5

What guidance does the Bible provide concerning how age should impact your ability to be useful? In most verses, the attainment of old age is seen as a blessing. However, little is mentioned about a term society usually associates with old age: "retirement." The concept that individuals over a certain age should retire is, in fact, a recent occurrence, brought about I expect by a longer lifespan and a higher standard of living. The term is only found in more recent translations of the Bible and then only once. The verse above from Numbers 8 applies only to priests serving in the temple. After age fifty they could still assist but were not to do the physical work. While you may retire from an earthly job, you should recognize that being a Christian is a lifetime occupation.

In Hebrews 12, you are told to run the race before you, and there is no mention that somehow you should not start because you view yourself too young or stop because you are *too old*. The verse from Psalms 92 is a reminder that the righteous will still be fruitful in their old age. In the final verse above, Paul reminds Timothy that he should not let others look down on him because of his age.

A search for additional Biblical guidance concerning age finds no reference that age alone should prohibit you from being useful. The only possible limit where age is concerned is the fact that those that are older may statistically have fewer years remaining to serve and may, as I am finding out recently, have some new physical limitations when it comes to lifting heavy loads. If you find yourself in this category, you may need to learn more about leverage and obtain some form of mechanized assistance. It may be time to buy a riding lawn mower and look for longer-handled tools. Notice I did not say you should stop mowing the lawn or using tools.

Perhaps I should include the following clarification. I know some 30-year-old individuals that probably should not mow grass or use tools, and I have known a few 90-year-old's who could do both. As always, where physical labor is concerned, use common sense and obey the guidance from your physician. Just do not use your age as an excuse to retire from life. Ultimately, you may turn some of the heavy work over to the younger generation as your physical abilities decline. That does not mean you retire from life or Christian service. Don't forget about the benefits technology provides in today's world to overcome what once were debilitating handicaps.

Your impact on the world and your family can be great regardless of your age if you allow yourself to be used by the Master. That should give those who are older a sense of urgency and those who are younger the desire to value the time available to serve. Remember, no one really knows how long they will live. You may have noticed, based on the daily news reports, youth is no guarantee of longevity.

Regardless of age, you are called to finish well and like the old plane continue to be useful. You will, after all, leave everything behind when you die. What will be your legacy?

Chapter 6 Questions

1. What excuses do older individuals use for not actively serving the Lord?

2. What excuses do younger people use for not actively serving the Lord?

3. What excuses do individuals that are between the age of 30 and 60 use for not actively serving the Lord?

4. Give examples of older and younger Christian you know who are actively serving the Lord.

5. What activity appeals most to you? If you are uncertain or have never thought much about it, pray that the Lord will show you a new place of service.

Chapter 7
Getting in Tune

In the past chapter, you learned that ultimately, age should not be a primary consideration for service or usability. However, you will find that age can impact the condition of your bargain priced tool simply because the older ones have had more time to get knocked around. Trying to use even a great tool that is in a bad condition can cause you to waste some of your precious time. In this chapter, you will learn how to improve the condition of a used tool while, at the same time, identifying an important Plane Truth.

So, what do you do once you are the new owner of a used plane that is showing the impact of years of neglect and misuse? The good news is that much of the ravages of time can be corrected if you are willing to invest the time and "elbow grease" effort. The process of rehabilitating a plane is commonly referred to as tuning. As you will learn later, even some new planes can benefit from a tune-up. When the process is finished, a used well-adjusted plane with a sharp blade makes a distinctive sound that is music to a woodworker's ears. Maybe that is why the process is called tuning. Or perhaps the name is analogous to the old automotive industry term for regular scheduled maintenance as in the phrase: "I need to take the car in for a tune-up."

Plane Truths for Living

Tuning consists of removing rust and dirt, flattening the sole of the plane, making sure any surface where there is metal to metal contact is flat and smooth, and sharpening the blade. Flattening the sole of the plane can be done a number of ways but always involves removing enough metal to ensure the bottom of the plane presents an extremely flat surface to the wood you are trying to plane. To the casual observer, all planes appear to have a flat sole. However, if you retract the blade and push the plane back and forth on a piece of sandpaper attached to a very flat surface, the high and low spots will immediately appear. The high spots will be the only ones made shiny by the sandpaper while the low spots will remain dull and unchanged in color. The picture below shows the before and after picture from a small block plane purchased in a bad condition at a flea market and restored to be a useful and functioning tool.

Before and After Pictures of simple Block Plane

If you are familiar with automotive engine rebuilding, you may recall that part of the process involves having a machine shop grind the engine head perfectly flat so that it mates up with the engine block for a tight leak-proof fit. In fact, you might be able to take the used plane to a machine shop and have the sole milled to make it flat. Since the cost of doing so usually exceeds the price paid for flea market planes, most woodworkers sand off the high spots by rubbing the sole of the plane on sandpaper attached to a very flat surface. The process starts with coarse (very rough to the touch) sandpaper and migrates to finer and finer grit until the bottom of the plane is flat and polished. Unless the sole is flat, you will not be able to consistently remove paper-thin wood shavings with each pass to flatten and smooth the board you are planing.

You might be surprised to learn that in some cases a shiny new plane out of the box could be functionally worse than a low-cost garage sale plane that has been properly tuned and maintained. This is because low-cost planes often come from the manufacturer with imperfections and design tolerances that dramatically reduce their functionality. If you have purchased a new lower quality plane, all is not lost. Making the sole flat and the other parts fit together can be a time-consuming process with the effort determined primarily by the amount of metal that needs to be removed. Looks can be deceiving when it comes to analyzing planes. As with individuals, being shiny on the surface may not tell you much about a plane's performance.

Plane Truth #6: From a human perspective, you should allow the Master Craftsman to clean you from the inside out.

Scriptures #6

"Cleanse me with hyssop[11] and I will be clean; wash me, and I will be whiter than snow." (Psalms 51:7)

---

11 Hyssop was the herb that was dipped in blood to mark the doorposts in Egypt to keep the angel of death from stopping at the Hebrew house (Ex 12:22) and is referred to numerous times in purification rites throughout the Old Testament. It was also the herb offered to Christ during the crucifixion (John 19:29). As such, David is asking God to purify him using the method the priests normally used.

"Create in me a pure heart O God, and renew a steadfast spirit within me." (Psalms 51:10)

"The sacrifices of God are a broken spirit; a broken and contrite heart, O God, you will not despise." (Psalms 51:17)

"The path of the righteous is level; O upright One, you make the way of the righteous smooth." (Isaiah 26:7)

"Consider it pure joy, my brothers, whenever you face trials of many kinds, because you know that the testing of your faith develops perseverance. Perseverance must finish its work so that you may be mature and complete, not lacking anything." (James 1:2-4)

"Therefore, get rid of all moral filth and the evil that is so prevalent and humbly accept the word planted in you, which can save you." (James 1:21)

Application #6

The first three verses above from Psalms, deal with letting God clean you up and create a heart that is in agreement with His. In Isaiah, you will find reference to the fact that righteousness, like your well-tuned plane, can create a smooth and level path. The first scripture from James is one of the harder verses in the Bible for most people to process because it says you should be grateful for trials so that in the end you may be mature and complete. I am pretty sure you have difficulty recognizing at the time that a trial will bring any benefit at all. During these times, it is helpful to remember Romans 8:28 states that all things work together for good for those that love God. Finally, in James 1:21 you are instructed to become moral and humbly accept God's word.

Being tuned by the Lord may require that He sand off some of the rough spots in your character, and at times that may be painful. Tuning also consists of allowing God to remove the rust, oil, and dirt you may have accumulated in your life. Just as a dirty out of tune plane is difficult to use and can't create a smooth surface, you can't be all you should be without being tuned by Him. While Plane Truth #1 dealt with the need for you to make the way straight and smooth for others, Plane Truth #6 concerns you as an individual.

Just like the well-tuned hand plane, if you are in tune, you will have less trouble creating a smooth surface for others. The purpose of tuning is not to improve the outward appearance of the plane, though removing the exterior grime will often do that. The purpose is to enable the plane to function according to the original manufacturer's specifications.

The Master knows what you are capable of and what you were designed to be. He looks beyond the rust and rough spots to see your real inner worth. In John 1:42 Jesus calls Simon to follow Him and changes his name to Peter. Later Jesus points out that the word Peter means "the rock" even though throughout Jesus' earthly ministry Peter was anything but a rock. He was often impulsive and did not support Christ during the trial and crucifixion. Christ looked beyond what Peter was to what he could become, and Peter went on to be a true rock and pillar of the early church.

Upon discussing this chapter with a friend, he reminded me of the writing of A.W. Tozer who wrote, *Praise God for the Hammer, the File and the Furnace.*[12] In his book Tozer points out that the hammer, the file, and the furnace are all implements that when viewed by the item being hammered, filed, or heated can seem to be cruel taskmasters. However, when you realize that both the hammer and the nail serve the same

---
12   A.W. Tozer, The Root of the Righteousness, 1955, page 76

master, it changes the perspective. In order to serve you may need to be hammered, filed, or heated. I encourage you to locate a copy of A.W. Tozer's full text on this subject and see if you do not agree it provides a deeper understanding of this chapter's Plane Truth.

Are you feeling out of tune from a spiritual perspective? Pray that the Lord will show you areas of your life that need improvement and provide guidance on how to change. Review the scripture verses from this section as you consider what the Lord would have you do.

Chapter 7 Questions

1. What areas of your life have you been keeping away from the Lord?

2. What do the scriptures listed earlier in this chapter teach you about the process of being tuned by the Lord? Locate and read through a copy of A.W. Tozer's writing on the hammer the, file, and the furnace. How does his writing relate to the scripture in James 1:2-4?

3. Compare and contrast the process of a woodworker looking for a used plane and how Christ looks at you?

4. Spend some time in quiet contemplation of what part you need to play in the tuning process and how you might begin to let the Lord tune you. During this time, consider what rough spots you need to have sanded down. We all have areas we would probably not put in writing or want to discuss in a group setting. Those are the principal areas you should consider bringing before the Master Craftsman.

Chapter 8
How Sharp Is Your Blade?

"If the ax is dull and its edge unsharpened, more strength is needed..." (Ecclesiastes 10:10)

In the previous chapter, a used hand plane was tuned to allow it to become a useful tool once again. One crucial step in tuning the plane was sharpening its blade. This chapter reviews the blade sharpening process in greater detail. As you might expect, blade sharpening will have human implications and lead you to identify a new Plane Truth.

The book of Ecclesiastes was written well over 2,000 years ago, and yet the verse above states a fact that is still important to us today. Just like the ax, a dull plane blade will cause you to work harder. You will also find that a dull blade produces a less satisfactory result. Unfortunately, if it is being used, even the sharpest blade does not stay sharp forever. This is true whether you have tuned a used plane or bought an expensive new one that needs no tuning. Therefore, if you want to be a less frustrated woodworker, you need to learn to sharpen your tools.

There are several ways to sharpen a blade, but all consist of removing steel and polishing the beveled edge with increasingly finer grits of some type of abrasive. Like the process of flattening the sole, sharpening the blade takes time even with mechanized sharpening equipment.

Plane Truths for Living

The effort required to sharpen a blade depends largely on its initial condition. If the previous owner failed to prepare the surface of the wood they were smoothing, the blade could have been damaged. Sharp blades do an excellent job of removing wood but come in second when faced with hidden nails, screws, and other items of metal. A sharp edge also does not deal well with an accidental fall to a concrete floor (please do not ask me how I know). Tools and jellied toast have a lot in common. They always seem to hit the floor in a manner producing the worst possible consequences. It also seems that if you drop a tool, it is often the one you just spent 20 minutes sharpening and not the dull one. The damage from nails, screws, and concrete floors usually produce a nick in the blade proportionate to the force with which the blade struck the object. Before the blade can be useful again, you will need to remove enough steel to make the nick disappear. Below is an example of a damaged blade I have on my "to be repaired later" list. The removal of these nicks will require a lot of sanding, thus the reason for it being done later—probably much later.

Result of Trying to Plane Wood with Embedded Nails

If the previous owner did not understand the proper angle or method of sharpening, even more steel may need to be removed. Plane blades are sharpened differently from knives and axes. The back side of a plane blade is always made as flat as possible, and most of the effort goes into sharpening the top side at a specific angle to the bottom. For smoothing planes, this angle is usually 25 degrees. If the past owner did not know this and attempted to sharpen the blade at a different angle or sought to sharpen the blade to a point by placing a bevel on both sides of the blade, you will have more work to do. The time and effort required to sharpen the blade properly is proportional to the degree of damage it has experienced. You will be glad to know that almost all blades can be sharpened. Rarely will a used plane require the purchase of a new blade.

As I mentioned earlier, blades must be sharpened with some form of abrasive. There are a broad range of options and costs where sharpening methods are concerned. The four most common are as follows: grinding wheels, flat rectangular stones[13] (referred to as water stones or oil stones based on what liquid should be placed on the surface of the stone to help with the sharpening process), flat metal plates with diamond chips embedded in them, or sandpaper attached to a very flat surface (thick plate glass is a favorite).

Unfortunately, there are no quick fixes to sharpening a blade. If you started with the fine grit sandpaper or stone, it might take days to sharpen the blade. Using the course grit first removes the most steel in the shortest period of t me and is the fastest way to produce a blade with the proper shape and angle. At the end of this first step, looking at the blade through a magnifying glass will reveal a surface with many scratches. As you reduce the coarseness of the abrasive material, the scratches will become smaller and smaller. It is surprising that the blade can't be really sharp until you get to the finest grit sandpaper or stone. Some woodworkers even use a very fine grinding powder on a

---

13   Sometimes referred to as whetstones.

leather strop[14] as the last step. At the completion of this final step, the blade should be sharp enough to shave with, and the surface will be as reflective as a mirror. Using a very sharp blade in your plane produces a smooth surface with the least amount of effort. One bit of good news concerning this process is that once a blade has been properly shaped and sharpened, it will require much less effort to sharpen when it becomes dull again.

Plane Truth #7: To be productive, you must submit to Christ and allow Him to file away the edge of your blade that has become rough or damaged as you struggle in the world.

Scripture #7

"No discipline seems pleasant at the time, but painful. Later on, however, it produces a harvest of righteousness and peace for those who have been trained by it." (Hebrews 12: 11)

"My son, do not despise the LORD's discipline and do not resent his rebuke, because the LORD disciplines those he loves, as a father the son he delights in." (Proverbs 3:11-12)

"Those whom I love I rebuke and discipline. So be earnest, and repent."(Revelation 3:19)

"Whoever loves discipline loves knowledge, but he who hates correction is stupid." (Proverbs 12:1)

---

14   A strop is a thick piece of leather to which fine grinding powder is applied. It is used in the final step of the sharpening process for a straight razor, knife or blade.

Application #7

After reading the four verses above, do you recognize how they relate to the writings of Tozer discussed in chapter 7? Remember the discipline provided by the hammer, the file, and the furnace. Had Tozer been a woodworker, I wonder if he would have added sandpaper and perhaps whetstone to his list.

Just like a poorly treated plane blade, past actions and bad decisions may have impacted your ability to be sharpened. The good news is that God can always repair you if you let Him open you up, remove the old dull blade of your life, and put a new edge on it. Through prayer, reading His Word, and fellowship with other believers, Christ can continue to polish and sharpen your life so that you can be used for His purposes. All blades, even those that are expensive with advanced design and a lot of potential become dull with use. Once they are no longer sharp, they are less and less efficient in removing wood and in extreme cases may even damage the project you are working on.

Sometimes the sharpening process is painful. Just as the blade for a hand plane may need to be reshaped by a grinding stone, you may be reshaped by something that causes you significant discomfort. Remember, the initial shaping of the blade required course grit sand paper or stones. Sometimes it takes God's discipline to get your attention and allow you to recognize you can't become sharp by just working harder. The plane blade will not get sharper as you plane more wood, just as working in your own strength will not sharpen your abilities.

Imagine a woodworker attempting to push a plane with a dull blade across a board. This not only requires a lot of physical effort but can be incredibly frustrating to the one doing the work. The plane may make a chattering sound as it digs into the wood and then releases. If this occurs, the surface of the wood will not be smooth. Now visualize the same woodworker with a well-tuned plane and sharp blade. The shavings of wood almost fly off the board, the product is beautiful to behold, and using the plane is much more enjoyable. You need the help of the Master to become truly sharp so that your life can be joyful and productive.

Chapter 8 Questions

1. What can cause your life to become ineffective like a dull blade in a hand plane?

2. Can a polished blade still be dull? How does this situation compare to people today?

3. If the blade in your plane has become dull, how will it impact your work and your finished product? Will using more force overcome the fact that the blade's dull?

4. What problems can be caused by Christians attempting to work in their own power?

5. To carry this analogy of sharpening a step further, what do you think it means to be sharpened spiritually? How do you think this is best accomplished?

6. Reread James 1:2-4 from the previous chapter. How does this verse relate to letting Christ sharpen you spiritually?

Chapter 9
What Is Your Blade Made Of?

Like peeling through the layers of an onion, are you continuing to observe the hand plane in greater detail? First, we improved and cleaned the basic parts of the plane. Then in the last chapter, we reviewed what it takes to create a very sharp edge. In this chapter, we analyze how a plane blade is made and discuss how often it requires sharpening.

Blades come in various grades of steel, thickness, and quality. Tool steel is tempered so that it will hold an edge and is an alloy[15] of several different materials depending on the blade's intended use. Some blade manufacturers even offer buyers two distinct types of steel as an option. Because of the material used and the method of tempering, manufacturers try to balance hardness with the ability to create a very sharp edge. As you increase hardness, the steel also becomes more brittle and the ability to have a sharp edge decreases.

An additional disadvantage of harder steel is that is takes more time to sharpen and will wear out your sharpening devices more quickly. Of course, the obvious advantage is that the edge you do create with this harder steel will last longer and increase the time between sharpening. Some craftsmen prefer a blade that requires less sharpening and

---

15 An alloy is usually created by melting two or more different metals together. For example when copper and zinc are combined they create an alloy we commonly think of as brass.

are willing to give up a slight reduction in the overall sharpness of the blade. These harder steel blades are tempered and designed with a composite material that can be made very hard. Others sharpen their blades more frequently and purchase a blade designed for the sharpest edge possible.

Woodworkers have a saying concerning when to sharpen a tool: "If you think it is time to sharpen your blade, you have probably waited too long between sharpening." The blade actually starts to become dull on the first cut. It then gradually becomes more and more dull. Because this happens over a period of time, you often fail to recognize you are working harder to get a quality product. Sharpening requires that you remove the blade and is, therefore, an interruption to your work. The desire to finish a project often causes you to attempt to continue without sharpening. "I will sharpen the blade before I do the next project," you tell yourself. Finally, something will happen, like a nick in your project or board, to remind you it is past time to sharpen. It is then you realize the blade has been dull for some time. Sharpening more frequently results in a better product and generates much less frustration.

Plane Truth #8: Being as sharp as possible requires that you return to the Master Craftsman frequently for sharpening. Long periods between sharpening result in a dull plane blade and with respect to your spiritual blade, a less effective life.

Scriptures #8

"Ever since the time of your forefathers you have turned away from my decrees and not kept them. Return to me, and I will return to you, says the Lord Almighty." (Malachi 3:7)

"Take my yoke upon you and learn from me, for I am gentle and humble in heart, and you will find rest for your souls." (Matthew 11:29).

"Let us not give up meeting together, as some are in the habit of doing, but let us encourage one another and all the more as you see the Day approaching." (Hebrews 10:25)

"How, then, can they call on the one they have not believed in? And how can they believe in the one of whom they have not heard? And how can they hear without someone preaching to them?" (Romans 10:14)

Application #8

If you look at Mark 5:3, you see Jesus is referred to by his neighbors as a carpenter. While the term carpenter[16] used in the Bible may have a broader meaning than today's definition, I often wonder if He would have used something like a hand plane in his work. From a more spiritual perspective, I would encourage you to consider Christ to be the Master Craftsman. Have you moved away from the Lord? In Malachi 3:7 you are told that all you need to do is return to Him. After all He has always been there waiting for you. In order to follow His instruction to "learn from me" in Matthew 11:29 above, you should consider yourself His apprentice.

To learn their skill, apprentice woodworkers and craftsmen of old were required to study under a master craftsman. The apprentice system seems to have started during the middle ages. Under this system, a young man or woman usually under the age of 21 interested in learning a trade was often indentured to a master craftsman. The craftsman pro-

---

16   The word translated as carpenter can also mean a builder or even a stone mason.

vided food, lodging, and training in a particular trade and the apprentice provided inexpensive labor. The training time period was often as long as seven years with the possibility of additional years of advanced training.

Just as woodworkers of the past apprenticed under a master craftsman, can you envision Christians being called to an apprenticeship with the true Master Craftsman—Jesus Christ? Instead of a seven-year commitment, serving Christ is a lifetime apprenticeship. Remember, no one would consider becoming an apprentice and then only visit the craftsman they served once a week for a couple of hours. The apprentice is in the shop each day, working and learning from the master. Daily attendance was mandatory, not optional.

Do you tend to forget the message from Hebrews 10:25 telling you that meeting together is essential? Paul reinforces this thought in Romans10:14 by reminding you of the need for preaching. Do you ever fall into the trap of trying to handle things on your own without spending time in prayer, study, or fellowship with other Christians?

Avoiding instruction is a lot like trying to fix a car without reading the repair manual. For example, if you have ever tried to fix an electric car window, you quickly discover that a seemingly simple task like removing the interior door panel becomes complicated without some guidance. The fact that you might have done this before on another car always seems of little use since manufacturers continue to change the way doors are constructed. Even if the procedure has not changed, you tend to forget at least one crucial step in the process. If you are persistent, you can remove the panel without a manual, but the chances are good something will be broken in the process. Replacing the panel after the window is repaired is problematic if it is broken. Holding the panel on with duct tape will work but will not impress your friends or your spouse and is not a great long-term solution.

The more talented you think you are, or perhaps the longer you have served the Lord, the easier it is to believe that you can do things on your own. In Matthew 10:24 Christ tells you, "*A student is not above his teacher, nor a servant above his master.*" Just like the plane blade, by the time you realize things are not going well, it is already too late. You then realize that you should have brought your problem to the Lord months ago. Your spiritual blade has become dull. You tried to solve your problem by working harder when what you really needed was sharpening.

So how do you sharpen your spiritual blade? Since the Bible is your owner's manual, you should study it regularly. It is always surprising how little humanity has changed over several thousand years, and how much great advice is contained within its covers.

Prayer is another important activity that helps keep you sharp. Remember, even Christ took time to pray. If Christ required time in prayer, why should you assume you can fight the daily battles without it? Spend time with the Master you are apprenticed to, so He can sharpen your spirit often and communicate with you through prayer. If you have difficulty setting aside the time, consider joining a prayer group to help you become accountable. If one is not available, ask your pastor for guidance in how to start one.

A good friend reminded me that all tools need other tools: tools to adjust, tools to clean, tools to sharpen, and tools to keep the blade aligned as it is sharpened These tools are not better or worse than the blade being sharpened; they just have different talents than the blade. Remember, "As iron sharpens iron, so one man sharpens another."

(Proverbs 27:17) Once the blade is in the proper shape, sharpening it the next time will be a much easier exercise. Sharpen often!

Chapter 9 Questions

1. What type of individual are you? Do you return to the Lord often for renewal or do you tend to try to handle things on your own?

2. Why do some of us fail to come before the Lord frequently?

3. What actions can you take to assist you in studying your owner's manual more often?

4. Can you think of other personal examples where a failure to obtain instructions has caused you problems?

Chapter 10

Where the Blade Meets the Wood

Chapter 9 explained the benefit of keeping your blade sharp. However, you will find that even a sharp blade will perform poorly if it is not properly inserted in a plane and adjusted to touch the wood. Before continuing, you may want to refer to the "Exploded View of a Smoothing Plane" in chapter 2 to help you visualize the parts of the plane being discussed.

From Chapter 2 you may recall that the opening in the sole of the plane that allows the blade to contact the wood is called the throat or mouth. The blade, frog, and mouth all work together to determine how much wood will be removed with each pass of the plane. Positioning the frog on the body of the plane controls how close the blade comes to the front of the mouth. The depth adjustment wheel and the lateral adjustment lever control the alignment of the blade on the frog.

Screws or Pins

Conventional planes fasten the frog to the base or sole of the plane with screws while more expensive planes utilize two pins. These screws or pins are underneath the blade at the front of the frog. Planes that use pins to hold the frog to the base allow you to incrementally move the frog back and forth by turning screws at the back of the frog. This configuration speeds up the adjustment process since it allows you to position the frog without removing the blade, chip breaker, and lever cap. The following picture shows the back of a plane designed with rear adjustment screws.

Back of Frog of a High-Quality Plane

Less expensive planes may have no screws or perhaps only one screw at the back of the frog. Adjustment for either the no-screw or the single screw arrangement requires the removal of the blade hardware and loosening the screws holding the frog to the body of the plane. Once the front screws are loosened, the single screw setup is a little easier to use than having no screw since the position of the frog can be moved forward or backward incrementally by turning the back screw. In either case, it is still a cumbersome trial and error process. After the frog is moved forward or backward, you must retighten the front screws, reinstall the blade, and check to see if the gap between the blade and the front of the mouth is correct.

Regardless of the configuration of the plane, the goal is to adjust the amount of blade exposed to the wood while moving the frog forward, reducing the gap between the front of the mouth and the blade's cutting surface. Correctly adjusted planes will show only a small gap between the blade and the front of the mouth and will enable thin shavings to be removed with each pass over the wood. If the gap is too large, the blade may have a tendency to tear the wood as opposed to shaving it, and will not leave a smooth surface.

The Frog

After the frog is properly positioned, the blade can be gradually advanced through the mouth by turning the depth adjustment wheel at the back of the frog. The more the blade is exposed, the thicker the shaving of wood.

Caution! For what should be obvious reasons, never run you finger over the sole of the plane to determine if the blade is properly adjusted. I mention this because I have found that things that are obvious in retrospect seem not to be in real time. More than a few woodworkers have determined too late that the blade is in fact extended and very sharp.

It is also helpful if the surface of the frog that the blade slides up and down on is as flat and smooth as possible. In some less expensive planes, the surface of the frog may be rough and uneven. This will make it harder to move the blace in and out smoothly in small controlled increments.

Lateral Adjustment

After the frog is adjusted and the blade is at its proper depth, the lateral adjustment lever is used to ensure the cutting edge is perpendicular to the sole of the plane. If this is not adjusted properly, ore corner of the blade will cut deeper than the other, creating a groove instead of a smooth surface.

Have you already guessed that the human mouth and the mouth on a plane have something in common?

Plane Truth #9: Keeping a tight mouth (a very small space between the blade and the front of the mouth) is required if you want to make thin controlled cuts. In your daily life you need to keep a tight mouth or "guard" your tongue and be careful what you say.

Scriptures #9

"The tongue has the power of life and death..." (Proverbs 18:21)

"He who guards his mouth and his tongue keeps himself from calamity." (Proverbs 21:23)

"My dear brothers, take note of this: Everyone should be quick to listen, slow to speak and slow to become angry. For man's anger does not bring about the righteous life that God desires." (James 1:19-20)

"The tongue also is a fire, a world of evil among the parts of the body. It corrupts the whole person, sets the whole course of his life on fire and is itself set on fire by hell." (James 3:6)

"Set a guard over my mouth, O Lord; keep watch over the door of my lips." (Psalms 141:3)

Application #9

Accurately adjusting a plane to reduce the space between the blade and the front of the mouth is not easy. Some of the difficulty is based on the design of the plane itself. For example, frogs lacking the unique capabilities found on more expensive planes require a more labor-intensive trial and error process for adjustment. While we all seem to have difficulty controlling our tongue from time to time, just like hand planes, some individuals may have more difficulty than others. If you know this is an issue for you, guard against situations that may cause you problems. The verse from the first chapter of James cautioning you to be slow to speak is of particular importance. Slowing down will give your brain time to catch up with your tongue. In the other four verses, two tell you to guard your tongue and two speak of the power the tongue has to get you in trouble.

If you search the Bible for similar instances where the actual word "tongue" is used, you will find at least 36 verses. When you expand your search to address the broader topic of speech you will find hundreds of additional verses. The fact that this is a repeating theme throughout the Bible should reinforce its importance to you as a topic for study. Remember, once said, your words cannot be unsaid.

Historically, we even have a saying from our agrarian past that relates well to the problem of words said in haste and a wish to call them back. Trying to retrieve your words "is like closing the barn door after the horse is gone."

When the books of the Bible were written, the spoken word was the primary source of communication. This spoken word was delivered face to face. While letters were also written in Jesus' time, they took weeks or months to deliver. This reliance on face to face spoken word continued to be the primary means of communications until a little over 100 years ago when telegraph and the telephone were invented. These two inventions began the advancements that brought us to the wide array of wired and wireless options we have today.

So why am I discussing advancements in telecommunications? Having spent a career in the communications industry, I must admit that it has always interested me. However, that interest is not why I brought up the subject. I did this to encourage you to grasp the deeper meaning of the scripture verses listed in this chapter and expand your view of the spoken word to encompass some of the modern options available for communication.

Remember, words can cause problems today even if they are not spoken. Various social media options allow you to respond to others quickly. This ability puts you in direct conflict with the directions in James 1:19; "be slow to speak." We all know of situations where email, social network entries, text messages, or tweets have been used to send responses far too quickly or to a wider audience than was intended. Perhaps a good paraphrase of the verse from Proverbs 21:23 for today's world should read, "He who guards his tweets and his smartphone keeps himself from calamity."

I suspect you know of at least one instance where an individual received an email sent to a large distribution list and then responded with what they thought was a private message to the person that sent the email. Unfortunately, they hit "Reply All" instead of "Reply." Much like an email sent to a wider audience than intended, words take on a life of their own once they are released. You can apologize, but the damage is already done. Repairing this damage, like that done by a misaligned woodworker's plane, is challenging and always time-consuming. It is much better to control what you say, or tweet, ahead of time than to try to repair the damage later.

Plane Truths for Living

Chapter 10 Questions

1. Review the five verses listed in this chapter. See if you can identify the context surrounding the scripture and provide a brief description of why you think each verse was written. Identify three reasons you think it is such a common topic.

2. How can you control your tongue?

3. Think back to times when you have said things you wished you hadn't. What caused you to speak improperly? What could you have done to avoid the problem?

4. Where politicians or individuals are concerned is there such a thing as "speaking off the record?" Give one example of where this has caused a problem.

5. Provide an example of where a tweet, email, or social media posting has caused unintended problems.

6. When making a posting, or sending an email or tweet, how long do you think about what you are doing before you hit send?

Chapter 11

Got Something "Stuck in Your Craw?"[17]

In the past chapter, you reviewed how the plane blade was adjusted to create a small space between the blade and the front of the mouth of the plane. If adjusted correctly it should provide a small space and allow fine shavings to be removed with each pass over the wood. Since the plane blade and the chip breaker (as shown in Chapter 2) are connected together under tension with a screw, they move together as you advance or retard the cutting edge. The chip breaker adds rigidity by reducing the flexing of the plane blade and directs the shavings away from the blade as they come through the mouth of the plane.

Occasionally a sliver of wood will become trapped between the chip breaker and the blade. This often occurs when you have some mechanical issue with the plane but it can happen even when everything appears to be positioned correctly. It can also occur if you mistakenly

---

17 A craw is a pouch in the throat of some birds that allows food to be predigested. When it exists, birds eat small pebbles or rocks that stay in the pouch and help break down the food. If something was eaten by the bird that was too large to be swallowed it could become stuck in the pouch. When my grandmother was experiencing some unresolved disagreeable or distasteful situation she would often say, "that _____ sticks in my craw."

plane a board in the wrong direction.[18] but sometimes it happens due to no apparent fault of the woodworker. Since the chip breaker and blade are fastened together under tension, and the top of the blade and the bottom of the chip breaker are both flat, there should be no gap between them. Therefore, it should be difficult for even a small piece of wood to get between them.

Visualize what it must look like to have a sliver of wood between the chip breaker and the blade. When this occurs, the sliver will block the path for additional wood to be cut and make its way through the section of the mouth where the blockage is located. Until the sliver is removed, you will not be able to use the plane effectively.

Once you have the problem, the sliver must be removed. If you are tempted to try to pull it out with a pair of pliers, stop. This approach poses some safety risks because you are working close to a very sharp blade. Also, you may dull the blade if the pliers bump into it. Finally, this approach may not be able to remove the piece of wood from the blade assembly completely. If any wood remains, it will create a gap between the blade and the chip breaker and will practically guarantee that new slivers will be picked up as soon as you begin to use the plane.

Correctly extracting the sliver requires that you remove the lever cap, separate the chip breaker and blade, remove the sliver, reassemble the blade and chip breaker, and replace the lever cap and blade assembly. Doing this is time-consuming, so may be tempted just to keep using the plane with the sliver in place since you are in a hurry to finish your project. In the long run trying to work around the problem will not produce a quality product and often creates more work for you. Below is an example of wood chips stuck between the blade and chip breaker.

---

18   A discussion concerning proper direction will be covered in the next chapter.

Slivers of Wood Trapped Between Blade and Chip Breaker

Once you have disassembled the blade and chip breaker, you should carefully examine them to ensure they fit tightly together without any gaps. If gaps exist, the leading edge of the chip breaker, where it meets the blade, may need to be ground to make it perfectly flat. If you have not recently sharpened the blade now is a good time to do that as well.

Plane Truth #10: Just like the plane, if you get something "stuck in your craw" as my grandmother used to say, you will have trouble dealing with people and responding to others as you should.

Scriptures #10

"Do not seek revenge or bear a grudge against one of your people, but love your neighbor as yourself. I am the Lord." (Leviticus 19:18)

"In your anger do not sin: Do not let the sun go down while you are still angry, and do not give the devil a foothold." (Ephesians 4:26-27)

"Therefore, if you are offering your gift at the altar and there remember that your brother has something against you, leave your gift there in front of the altar. First go and be reconciled with your brother; then come and offer your gift." (Matthew 5:23-24)

"See to it that no one misses the grace of God and that no bitter root grows up to cause trouble and defile many." (Hebrews 12:15)

Application #10

It is never good to let problems remain unresolved or allow them to fester. Have you ever gotten a splinter under your fingernail? It is surprising how much it hurts, even if the splinter is tiny. Left alone, a small splinter can still impact your ability to work. Given sufficient time, a splinter can even cause an infection. Like properly removing the sliver between the blade and chip breaker, it is always best to remove the splinter in your finger as soon as possible. Unaddressed issues and bitterness between individuals usually cause relationships to get worse and worse over time.

The first two scriptures listed for this chapter should remind you that love should counteract revenge and that carrying anger can get you into trouble. We have all seen the terrible consequences of anger and revenge. While these two forces have created much pain and suffering throughout human history, you do not have to look any further than the nightly news to find current examples of their devastating impact. In the second verse, you are instructed not to let the day end while you are angry. Since you obviously cannot control the length of the day, how should you respond to this command?

The third scripture shows that not only can a lack of resolution cause a problem between individuals, but it can impact your fellowship with your Heavenly Father. In this scripture from the book of Matthew, Jesus tells you to take the first step to resolve any differences between you and a brother. In this case, Jesus says if you remember that someone has something against you. That is if someone is angry with you. The scripture does not say if the anger they hold for you is justified or if you are also angry with them. You are told that Christ expects you to attempt reconciliation even if you do not think you are in the wrong. Why do you think Christ instructs you to leave the altar and address another's anger? Could it be because He knows the danger of letting anger in another fester? Note that Christ does not instruct you to stay at the altar and pray about the problem.

While you may think that unresolved differences and anger only impact the two people immediately involved in the issue, you will learn that they will ultimately affect a far greater audience. Whole families and future generations can be impacted if the situation remains unresolved. I am sure you have heard stories or known of individuals who carried a grudge and bitterness against someone for a lifetime, creating pain for themselves and others. This fact was reinforced by a situation my family once encountered.

We had moved into a house in Connecticut after a job initiated relocation from Texas. The seller had been the original owner and commented that his family hated to leave, but a similar job situation was requiring them to move to Florida. About a year after the move, one of our kids found a silver spoon in the flowerbed. Noticing that the spoon was sterling silver and appeared to be part of a set, we mailed a note to the previous owners asking if it might be theirs.

A week later we received a heart-rending letter thanking us and saying yes, the spoon was theirs and could we please mail it to them.

It turned out that the spoon had first been missed after the visit of a relative. The lost spoon caused a problem in their family because they thought the relative had stolen it. Evidently, a bitter argument had ensued, and the family members had not spoken to each other since the incident. We mailed the spoon to Florida with our sincerest hope they were able to reconcile their problems. Like trying to retract words that have been said, this story shows that it is difficult to turn back time.

Holding a grudge impacts all individuals involved. It is surprising how often a grudge begins as a simple misunderstanding. To make matters worse, the problem may only be based on the facts as you think you know them and not on what actually occurred.

Christ instructs you to be different from the world. If you are currently in a situation that requires your forgiveness, remember Christ forgave you, and you are called to forgive others. (Matthew 6:14-15) "For if you forgive men when they sin against you, your heavenly Father will also forgive you. But if you do not forgive men their sins, your Father will not forgive your sins."

I have had people tell me that it was simply not humanly possible for them to forgive a wrong done to them. Forgiving or asking for forgiveness is not something that comes naturally to any of us. It requires Christ's love living in and through us. (Colossians 3:15) "Let the peace of Christ rule in your hearts since as members of one body you were called to peace." Review all the scriptures in this chapter as they relate to conflict between you and others. If you have something stuck in your craw, pray that the Lord will show you how to remove it.

Chapter 11 Questions

1. Has an acquaintance or family member, ever had had something "stuck in their craw?" Has it been resolved?

2. If you do not have the issue today, what are some actions you can take to insure you do not create a situation in the future?

3. Can you think of an example where a misunderstanding caused a problem? How could the problem have been avoided? Was it resolved? If so how?

4. How has holding a grudge impacted the holder of the grudge? Can the impact cause physiological problems? What impact does it have on family and acquaintances?

Chapter 12
The Angle and Direction of Attack Is Important

Now that you have a sharp blade and all the problems between the blade and the chip breaker have been resolved, it is time to examine the design of the hand plane more closely and observe how it is used by the woodworker. To better understand a hand plane's operation, you will need to know something about the wood you are working on and how this basic raw material for furniture making came to be.

You have probably seen the growth rings on a cross section of a tree that has been cut down and heard how the rings reveal a tree's age. During a trip to Yosemite, we toured a stand of giant Sequoias and viewed an example of tree rings that demonstrated some of the trees were several thousand years old. From a woodworking perspective, tree rings impact the wood you use and the approach you take when using a plane.

To create lumber, the saw at the mill cuts along the length of the tree trunk, slicing through the rings. These cut rings reveal the wood's grain and are the reason each individual board displays a unique pattern. This design will vary depending on how straight the tree was, any imperfections or forks it had, and whether the board is cut from the outside or middle of the trunk. The darker lines on these boards are the visible part of the rings that were cut through by the saw. Boards from the outside edge of the trunk have a wide space between the individual darker lines and often display a "V" shaped pattern on the surface. Those cut from near the center of the tree show the grain much closer together and usually has a more consistent pattern.

If you look at the surface of a piece of wood, you can see that it represents multiple layers. It is this uniqueness in wood grain that gives a piece of wood and ultimately the furniture made from it much of its beauty. When examining the surface and edge of a board, you can determine the directions these layers take to arrive at the surface of the lumber. In some cases, you may even be able to feel the difference. One direction will seem smooth to the touch while the other direction may be rough. This roughness comes from the feel of pushing against the ends of the wood fibers as they exit the surface of the wood.

When using a hand plane, it is important to determine the direction of the wood fibers and always try to plane (cut) with the grain. If you don't, the plane blade will tend to lift up the fibers tearing them off instead of cutting them smoothly. The woodworking term for the problem this produces is aptly called "tear-out." As we learned in the past chapter, planing against the grain may also cause the slivers that are lifted up to be wedged between the chip breaker and the blade. One way to remember the proper direction is to equate planing against the grain with rubbing a cat's fur from tail to head. This does not produce a very good result for the cat or the individual doing the petting.

In addition to the proper direction, the angle at which the blade contacts the wood is also important and will be different depending upon the design of the plane and its intended use. The No. 3 smoothing plane discussed in the introduction and in Chapter 2 is designed so that the cutting edge will contact the wood at 45 degrees. This angle is the combined result of the shape of the frog and the blades' cutting edge. The 45-degree angle is utilized on most smoothing and joiner planes. Low angle planes meet the surface at an even smaller angle (37 degrees or less) and are often used when planing end grain (end of a board across the grain). The blade of a number 80 cabinet scraper discussed in Chapter 4 contacts the wood at an even higher angle than 45 degrees and can remove very fine wood shavings. Its high angle of attach is particularly suited to surfacing wood in which the grain does not consistently go in one direction. There are many wood planes available, and each one has been designed to solve a particular woodworking problem.

    Understanding the surface of a piece of wood is of vital importance when it comes to selecting the correct plane and using it correctly. Even with practice, determining the direction of the grain is not always easy since it may occasionally change direction as you move from one end of the board to the other. This problem is more common if the tree the board was cut from contained a fork or had some outside influence change the direction of its growth. The more irregular the grain, the harder it is to work properly. Creating a smooth surface on a piece of wood whose grain changes direction frequently requires a cautious approach and may call for the use of special planes. The good news is that wood with constantly changing grain (sometimes referred to as burled or highly figured wood) can be used to create beautiful end products if the grain is properly understood. How does this discussion of wood grain apply to your interpersonal relationships?

Plane Truth #11: People respond best to an approach that fits their personality or gifts and talents. Otherwise, the result could be a tear-out in some of life's most important relationships.

Scripture #11

"Though I am free and belong to no man, I make myself a slave to everyone, to win as many as possible. To the Jews I became like a Jew, to win the Jews. To those under the law, I became like one under the law (though I myself am not under the law), so as to win those under the law. To those not having the law, I became like one not having the law (though I am not free from God's law but am under Christ's law), so as to win those not having the law. To the weak I became weak, to win the weak. I have become all things to all men so that by all possible means I might save some." (1 Corinthians 9:19-22)

Application #11

The concept of wood grain was so well understood in the past that a common saying evolved which is still with us today: "You are trying to go against the grain." As most of you understand, this saying describes an individual who has taken a path that seems sure to have obstacles.

Most woodworkers learn the principles concerning wood grain early in their training. However, there is always the temptation to take a shortcut. While working with a hand plane, you might think it is too much trouble to turn the board or reverse the direction you are planing in order to work with the grain. After all, your blade is sharp, you are really good at this, and what's more, you tell yourself, "think of the time I will save." If you approach a project in this manner, or if you use the wrong plane for a given woodworking task, the chances are good you will not be successful and may end up ruining a beautiful, and perhaps expensive, piece of wood.

Where interpersonal relationships are concerned, you should reflect on the concept discussed in this chapter and remember Paul's comments from his first letter to the Corinthians. Attempt to understand the individuals with whom you interact. If possible, try to change your approach to fit the individual and the situation.

Like boards with changing grain patterns, individuals can also be unique and complex. Much like a tree, personalities have also been shaped by historical or external conditions. This complexity may make some harder to judge than others. Remember, you can't always tell a book by its cover.

Have you ever met someone and formed a first impression that ultimately proved to be false? To avoid making a mistake that places you in an "against the grain" situation, it's best to build an initial relationship based on something you both have in common. Paul used his own life experiences to allow him to relate to others. He was Jewish, and grew up learning the scriptures and understood what it meant to be "under the law." However, he was also a Roman citizen which allowed him to better understand and communicate with those outside of Judaism.

After his conversion experience on the road to Damascus (Acts 9:3-19), he understood that salvation was not based on rigidly obeying a set of laws. Therefore, he could also speak to those that were not Jewish and had no prior knowledge of the law. Finally, he was referred to as someone who was small in stature (2 Corinthians 10:10) and commented about a thorn in the flesh (2 Corinthians 12:7) that kept him humble. Therefore, when he spoke to those who were viewed as weak he could also relate to them.

Plane Truths for Living

When you meet someone for the first time, remember the Plane Truth from this chapter and work to create a smooth relationship. Determine the direction of their grain. Remember, the hand plane will remove wood in either direction. However, only one direction will result in a smooth surface.

Chapter 12 Questions

1. Did Paul mean that you should violate your principles or your beliefs when dealing with others?

2. Do you have acquaintances at work or in your neighborhood who you have difficulty relating to? How can you change your approach to be able to communicate with them?

3. A source of conflict in many churches today is the style of music. What do you think Paul's suggestion would be to those experiencing the conflict on either side of the issue? What is the purpose of worship?

4. The most challenging piece of wood or the one with the most unique grain pattern often ends up being the most beautiful end product. Can you think of any examples where this principle might apply to difficult individuals?

Chapter 13

Collectible versus Usable

Congratulations, you have completed more than half of the book. Do you feel you have a better understanding of the construction and operation of the woodworker's hand plane? I hope you have also benefited from the Plane Truths these hand tools have led you to discover. Previous chapters analyzed how planes are designed, cleaned, tuned, and sharpened. You have even learned, as we discussed in the past chapter, that the surface of the wood will impact your work. The next six chapters will use your newfound knowledge to identify Plane Truths based on a more global analysis of woodworkers and their planes. For example, this next chapter asks the question: "Why do woodworkers purchase planes in the first place?" I initially thought the answer to this question would be obvious. However, I soon learned that not everyone buys a plane for practical reasons. I suspect you may also be surprised by some of the answers to this question.

Why would you purchase a hand plane? I can think of at least four reasons.

First, you may, of course, buy one because of its ability to remove small amounts of wood from a project and to make rough boards smooth. If the item is well-made and properly tuned, it will continue to have value and provide a return on your investment should you decide to sell it in the future.

Second, even if you have two or more of an item, you never know when you might need a spare. As you learned earlier in the book, some individuals have more than one of a particular tool simply because they forgot what they already owned. Even when this happens, they seldom sell or attempt to return the second or third item.

Third, you might purchase it to share with someone else. I have also noticed one curious fact. While woodworkers hardly ever sell their extra tools, it is not uncommon for them to give away a tool now and then. This is especially so if done in the process of inducting a neophyte into the world of woodworking. Woodworkers, after all, are generally a generous lot. Having said this, I should make one thing perfectly clear: "No, you cannot have my Bedrock plane."

Fourth, you might buy a plane for its artistic value. These collectible tools are often purchased to look at rather than use since using them could create scratches or place fingerprints on their shiny surfaces. My friend Dave has coined a term for these planes. "Oh. You're talking about a 'shelf plane,'" he once told me, when I asked about a particular company that manufactures planes noted for their beauty, quality, and price. At first, I thought he had misunderstood me since I was wondering what type of plane would be used specifically to make shelves. Recognizing the puzzled look on my face, he explained that some planes are purchased for the purpose of sitting on a shelf or in a display cabinet. Many are made with combinations of brass, iron, and exotic inlaid hardwoods. In addition to their good looks, they are also excellent tools with flat surfaces and sharp blades. An Internet search confirmed that they frequently receive high marks for design and function in comparative analysis tests. However, many of the individuals who own them seldom if ever put them to use.

To preserve these collectible planes and perhaps ensure they maintain their value, owners frequently keep them stored in the box in which they were shipped. This is a common practice in that it demonstrates that the plane was well cared for. When you look at these shipping boxes, you may also discover that they are often uncommon boxes. Some collectible planes ship in nicely designed hardwood boxes packaged inside cardboard shipping boxes. For example, one vendor makes the boxes for planes out of walnut, and they are beautifully finished. Not only are the planes stored where they cannot be easily observed, they are covered up by a pretty exterior. The boxes contain foam padding with cut-outs just to fit the shape of the plane to keep it safe from any possible damage during shipping. In order to see their beauty, you must take the box off the shelf and open it up.

Even though these planes are beautiful, comfortable to hold, and excellent at performing the cutting functions planes are designed for, many woodworkers are hesitant actually to use them. One slip or careless action that knocks them to the floor of your shop could dramatically reduce the value of a costly tool. These planes often sell for $500 to more than $1,000 depending on the type.

Picture a beautiful tool sitting on a shelf, designed to do a task that it is never going to do. Does that seem a little sad? It does to me. If I were more of an artist, perhaps I would have a better appreciation for the shelf plane. To placate my artist friends and maybe my friend Dave as well, I must admit that I do appreciate the beauty of a well-designed plane. I enjoy holding it and looking at it, but with regard to planes of the type just described, I might also be too scared of damaging it actually to put it to use.

While thinking about shelf planes, I came face to face with the realization that many of us have a lot in common with them. Do you have anything in common with a shelf plane? Shelf planes have a lot of potential, but all that potential is seldom put to use. Since they spend most of their time on display, they rarely create anything. Observing these collectible planes with so much potential sitting on a shelf just seems "wrong." As mentioned earlier, some shelf planes aren't even on display for others to look at since they are stored safely inside a container of some type. When you visualize shelf planes sitting on display or in storage, do the following new plane truths come to mind?

Plane Truth #12: In today's world, you are designed for service and not to sit on a shelf. Don't be a "Shelf Christian."

Plane Truth #13: Even if you are active inside a church, do not hide your light inside a nice-looking church building. You are called to get out of the box and have an impact on a far larger geography.

Scriptures for #12 and #13

"You are the light of the world. A city on a hill cannot be hidden. Neither do people light a lamp and put it under a bowl. Instead, they put it on its stand, and it gives light to everyone in the house. In the same way, let your light shine before men, that they may see your good deeds and praise your Father in heaven." (Matthew 5:14-16)

"Suppose a brother or sister is without clothes and daily food. If one of you says to him, "Go, I wish you well; keep warm and well fed," but does nothing about his physical needs, what good is it?" (James 2:15-16)

"But the man who had received the one talent[19] went off, dug a hole in the ground and hid his master's money." (Matthew 25:18)

"And throw that worthless servant outside into darkness where there will be weeping and gnashing of teeth." (Matthew 25:30)

"Therefore go and make disciples of all nations, baptizing them in the name of the Father and of the Son and of the Holy Spirit, and teaching them to obey everything I have commanded you. And surely I am with you always, to the very end of the age." (Matthew 28: 19-20)

"But you will receive power when the Holy Spirit comes on you; and you will be my witnesses in Jerusalem, and in all Judea and Samaria, and to the ends of the earth." (Acts 1:8)

Application #12

Are you a "Shelf Christian," all dressed up on Sunday for the world to see thinking; "But please do not ask me to do anything at the church, serve on a committee, or participate in an activity outside of Sunday morning"? If you tend to be a "Shelf Christian" you need to remember that we are called to let our light shine and to be useful.

---

19 In the Old Testament, the word translated talent was a unit of measure or weight. That is, people referred to a talent of silver to indicate a certain amount of silver by weight. By Jesus' time the Greek word "talanton," translated as "talent" in most English Bibles, was used to indicate a large sum of money. The word we use today to indicate a skill or ability comes from this Greek word.

Plane Truths for Living

Recognize that you may be the best example of a Christian some people know. In the first verse listed above, Jesus is talking about the light being the knowledge you have of Christ and His salvation. Jesus did not say that people should see *your* light and say how beautiful your light is or how bright you shine or even how much light you produce. The world often views success by how one is perceived by others. From the world's perspective, it is all about *you*. The Bible says it is not all about you; it is all about CHRIST. He said the light should show your good deeds so that those that see them will praise the Father and not the individual that did the deeds. Remember, from scripture verse 6 in Chapter 3 associated with Plane Truth 1, Ephesians 2:10 states that God has even prepared these deeds for us to do.

A shelf plane has never smoothed a board, has never worked to build a beautiful piece of furniture and therefore has no works to show. All a shelf plane has to show is itself. A shelf Christian like a shelf plane has no deeds for people to see. If there are no deeds, how can others see your light and glorify your Father?

Are you one who hears the Word on Sunday, learns about God's will, and has a lot of potential, but never really puts your light into practice? God has called you to be productive and not put on a show. If bringing attention to yourself is what makes you happy and is all that motivates you, the Bible points out that the praise of men is ALL you will receive (Matthew 6:2) "So when you give to the needy, do not announce it with trumpets, as the hypocrites do in the synagogues and on the streets, to be honored by men. I tell you the truth, they have received their reward in full."

Shelf Christians also seem to change their personalities when they get inside the church. During the week, few sit on shelves. They are very involved in the world and in their chosen profession. They are gifted in many areas and have no trouble using those gifts. In fact, that is how they earn their living. When it comes to church and Christian activities, do you fail to make use of your abilities and skills that earn you a living the other five or six days of the week? Remember, God has called you to be a good steward of ALL you have been given.

The first two scripture verses previously listed in this chapter should encourage you to let your light shine. The third verse provides as an example of a man who, after being made responsible for administering his master's money, decided the best way to protect it was to hide it. Just like the servant who was given money, Christians have received a gift worth far more than money. We have the message of God's grace, forgiveness, and salvation. If we do not share it with the world, we are like the servant who hid the gift he was given. You can see in the fourth verse it did not end well for him.

The scripture in the fifth and sixth verses above indicates Jesus commands us to "go and make disciples" and to "be my witnesses." The message Christians have been entrusted with is more valuable than gold or silver and is meant to be shared not hidden.

Application #13

Are you busy in a church but hiding inside the building? If you have gotten off the shelf but are still in the box, you need to broaden your horizons. It is important to receive training while enjoying the fellowship of other believers. You should attend services and contribute to the operation of the church. As previous lessons have indicated, you will have difficulty staying spiritually sharp without these activities. However, if you are only letting your light shine inside a nice-looking box you call the church, is your light really shining for the ones who need it outside the church?

From the perspective of the plane, the inside of the box is really nice. It is protected, secure, and free from the problems of the world. Like the church, it feels safe and secure, and certainly, it should. Just do not become so focused on the inside of the box that you forget there is a world outside that also needs to hear the message and see the light.

Chapter 13 Questions

1. Have you ever heard of the 80/20 rule? What does it mean? Does this rule apply in any churches you know?

2. What are some deeds that would lead people to praise God?

3. Why do you think people have few deeds that would lead people to praise God?

4. Do you think the scripture in Matthew 5:13 relates to this discussion? If so, how?

5. Does the analogy above remind you of any situations you or those you know have experienced?

6. Review Matthew 25:14-30. Identify four main points identified in these verses. How does this parable relate to your life today?

7. How does the example of a plane inside a box relate to Matthew 5:15?

Chapter 14
Analysis Paralysis or the Fear Factor

An individual at my former job always seemed to have great difficulty finishing a project. No matter what he was given, there was never enough information to complete a report, make a recommendation, or order the work to begin. In business, we had a saying for that situation. It was called "analysis paralysis." This occurs when you let the overall analysis process paralyze your ability to finish the work. The paralysis can impact individual workers, committees, or even entire companies.

I am aware of one product by a large national company that has been in the planning stage for over five years and still has not been deployed. A recent check of the status revealed that changing technology has made the project obsolete, and the window of opportunity has probably closed. Literally millions of dollars were spent on a project that never generated a dime of revenue.

These analysis paralysis groups or companies were sometimes referred to as "Ready, Aim" groups (from the old military saying – Ready, Aim, Fire) because they could never seem to say the word "Fire." They would get ready; they would aim, and then decide the situation was just not right to start the project. They might even get far enough along to deploy a small market trial, but then identify problems that sent the project back into the planning stage.

Sometimes woodworkers are like that. Usually, it concerns an expensive or unique piece of wood. Curly maple is a light-colored wood that has wavy highlights. When properly finished these bands almost appear to move as you look at them from different angles. I purchased a piece of curly maple three years ago, and to this day it is still in the attic of my shop. It is not for lack of projects that it sits there as I have completed several pieces of furniture since I purchased this wood.

The problem from a woodworking perspective is actually threefold:

1) First, it is such a great piece of wood you that end up telling yourself you are waiting for a project worthy of its use to come along. To date, my particular piece of wood has not gotten past the *worthy project* phase.

2) Once you get by the *worthy project* phase, the wood may sit on your bench for weeks without being touched by a saw or plane for fear you might ruin it. The wood in this example has simply become *too pretty* to cut. Perhaps you could call this wood *shelf wood* since it is similar to the shelf plane and is never used for its intended purpose. You can make up all kinds of excuses for why the project has not been started. Perhaps another piece of wood would be better for this project. Or what if you get in the middle of the project, don't have enough wood to finish and can't find anything that matches. Or what if your saw blade is not quite sharp enough and creates a problem. Perhaps you should wait until you change the saw blade or until you have just finished sharpening the blade on your hand plane. The excuses can be endless but the truth is you are afraid things will not turn out as you hope and it seems safer

to wait. If you get by this phase and the project is finally built, you still are not free of analysis paralysis.

3) The third stage of delay concerns the finish that is applied to the wood. Should you use a stain, a dye, or add no color at all? If you decide to use a stain, what color is best? What if the wood does not stain uniformly? Is the surface planed or sanded smooth enough? What finish should you use after it is stained—should you use an oil, shellac, varnish, or polyurethane? How many coats of finish should you use?

Just like the woodworker, the Bible and our everyday world contain many examples of human paralysis. The Children of Israel were initially afraid to enter the Promised Land. It took them 40 years to learn that with God all things, including conquering *giants* and crossing raging rivers, are possible. Jonah ran from the Lord, and it took spending quality time with a whale before he agreed to do what God had formerly commanded.

Plane Truth #14: The Lord has great plans for you, but you must not let fear control your actions.

Scriptures #14

"Why did you stay among the campfires to hear the whistling for the flocks? In the districts of Reuben there was much searching of heart. Gilead stayed beyond the Jordan. And Dan, why did he linger by the ships? Asher remained on the coast and stayed in his coves. The people of Zebulun risked their very lives; so did Naphtali on the heights of the field. "(Judges 5:16-18)

"Joshua told the people, "Consecrate yourselves, for tomorrow the Lord will do amazing things among you." Joshua asked the priests, "Take up the ark of the covenant and pass on ahead of the people." So they took it up and went ahead of them." (Joshua 3:5-6)

"Now the Jordan is at flood stage all during harvest. Yet as soon as the priests who carried the ark reached the Jordan and their feet touched the water's edge, the water from upstream stopped flowing. It piled up in a heap a great distance away over opposite Jericho... The priest who carried the ark of the covenant of the Lord stood firm on dry ground in the middle of the Jordan, while the whole nation had completed the crossing on dry ground." (Joshua 3:15-17)

"For I know the plans I have for you, declares the Lord, plans to prosper you and not to harm you, plans to give you hope and a future." (Jeremiah 29:11)

"For you did not receive a spirit that makes you a slave again to fear, but you received the spirit of sonship..." (Romans 8:15)

Application #14

From a woodworking perspective, fear can keep you from being creative and from enjoying something you might have created. Fear of failure is not unique to those of us in the 21st century. The verses above show that many Old Testament individuals and groups suffered from a fear of failure. That fear often meant they were reluctant to commit to actions they perceived as a risky.

The first scripture listed above is from a song of victory related to the involvement of the Israelite prophetess Deborah in the 12th century BC.[20] Though the prophetess ordered Barak to attack Sisera to free Israel from oppression, not all the Israelites quickly answered the call to participate. Many in Ruben's tribe are referred to as having "much searching of heart" while those from the tribe of Gilead, Dan, and Asher simply seemed to be waiting. Have you ever approached a situation with "much searching of heart?" I think today we would have said they were indecisive. You should always ask for spiritual guidance, but you should not use that excuse for lengthy delay. Note that the tribes did not state they would not participate. They simply did nothing. Also, note that in the second and third set of verses no miracles occurred until Joshua and the Israelites committed themselves to God, and the priests acted on that consecration by getting their feet wet.

When you let fear and a failure to trust in the Lord keep you from acting, you rob yourself of the blessings God has for you. This does not mean you should act foolishly, against godly counsel, or without the guidance of the Holy Spirit. It does mean that whenever the Lord leads you to move, you should act promptly. Failure to act is not to say that God's plans are put on hold. It may mean that someone else receives the blessing you might have received had you acted promptly.

The good news is that God does have a plan for you. The fourth set of verses above is from a letter of direction Jeremiah provided to the children of Israel who had been carried off to exile in Babylon. They were demoralized, living without a sense of purpose. and would have very likely ceased to exist as a nation had they not taken Jeremiah's message to heart. Is verse four only intended for the Israelites of thousands of years ago? It does show the heart of God toward his children. I prefer to view it as an Old Testament complementary verse to the New

---

20   The complete story is found in Judges Chapters 4 and 5. Warning, parts of this story may not be suitable for younger audiences.

Testament scripture in Romans 8:28 "And we know that in all things God works for the good of them who love him, who have been called according to his purpose."

A chapter concerning the impact of fear of failure on individuals would not be complete without the fifth verse. It should remind you that with Christ, you no longer need to be a slave to fear.

Chapter 14 Questions

1. Do you think the Israelites experienced a fear of failure? If so how did they overcome it? If not, why not?

2. Can you give any examples of how the Lord has acted in your life or the life of others at just the right time?

3. What are some of the fears that keep you from completing a task?

4. Read John 20:3-8. Does this passage relate to Plane Truth #14? If so how?

5. What does the following sentence mean? "God is always on time, but He is hardly ever early." Is this a true statement? How does this relate to this chapter on analysis paralysis?

6. How can you know something is God's will? What part does the Bible, prayer, godly counsel of others, and everyday life play in understanding God's will?

Chapter 15
Power Made Perfect in Weakness

Now let's return to the story of the tool show in the rain and the purchase of the "silk purse" plane that started me down the path to writing this book. As previously mentioned, the tool I bought was a Fulton Plane. I could tell it was manufactured under the Fulton brand because they neatly stamped the name Fulton and the number 3709 on the side of the plane. The use of a four-digit number beginning in 3 seemed to be a standard method Sears used to categorize some of their tools. This fact and the name Craftsman on the lever cap (see exploded view in Chapter 2) led me to believe that Fulton made the plane for Sears. Lever caps are pretty interchangeable, so there is no way of knowing for sure if the cap is really the original. Below you will find two pictures of the "silk purse" plane.

From the size of its base it was indeed a No. 3 plane, and at first glance was very similar to a No. 3 plane I already owned. The exploded view picture of a plane shown in Chapter 2 is a No. 3 Stanley plane. Yes indeed, you read correctly, it appears that I had purchased a duplicate of something I already owned. I really must start carrying a list of my tool inventory with me when I go shopping. Not only that, this plane

Plane Truths for Living

Fulton No. 3 Smoothing Plane

Brand Label on Side of the Smoothing Plane

was functionally lower in quality than the one I already owned. The back of the frog did not have any screws, and as discussed in Chapter 10, which would make adjustments difficult. On the next page is a picture of the back of the Fulton frog. You can see this plane has a relatively basic design.

Undaunted by the fact that I had just purchased a plane my wife might think was unnecessary, I justified it based on a rule Dave taught me: "everyone can use a spare." I also thought to myself, "The blade alone is probably worth the price of the plane, and I could just discard the Fulton or use it for parts and put the shiny new blade in the Stanley No. 3."

Back of the Frog on the Fulton Plane

This blade and chip breaker were not manufactured by Stanley or Fulton. They came from a current day company renowned for making high-quality planes and woodworking tools. A search of this modern-day company's website revealed that the blade and chip breaker combination would cost over $65 if purchased today. This new-found knowledge made the purchase of a second, probably unneeded, No. 3 plane a little easier to take. The following picture shows the blade, chip breaker and lever cap. This hardware is far superior to the blade that originally came on either a Stanley No. 3 or the Fulton plane. The blade is thicker, and the chip breaker is of a unique design.

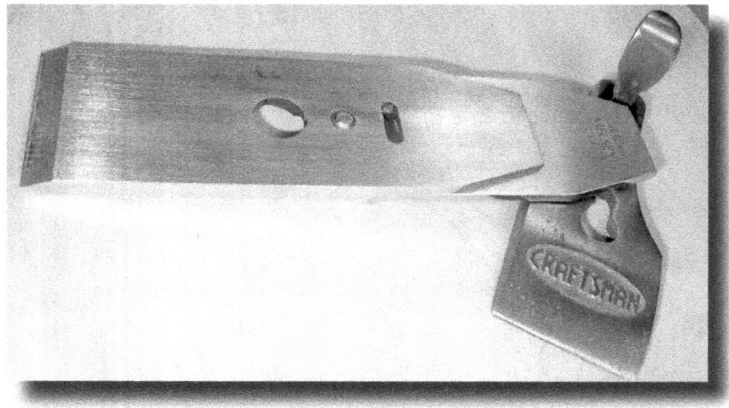

New Blade, Chip Breaker, and Craftsman Lever cap

If I had not still been experiencing the euphoria of purchasing a new (used) plane, I would have probably asked myself why someone would buy an expensive blade for this lower functionality plane. At this point, I thought my problem had been solved and headed to the shop to exchange blades and move on. Once in the shop, I removed the blades and lever caps from the Fulton and Stanley planes and attempted to install the shiny new blade in my No. 3 Stanley. I say "attempted" because try as I might, the new blade would not extend through the sole of the Stanley plane far enough to contact any wood.[21] Since I had hoped to use the plane for something more than a storage device for a blade, I loosened the Stanley frog and made numerous attempts to adjust it to provide more space.

After thirty minutes of high-level *under my breath* mumbling while working with the blade, chip breaker, and frog, it became apparent that this blade was simply not going to work in the Stanley plane. It was the same width and length as the one that had initially come in the Stanley, so what was the problem?

---

21   While you would agree this configuration would cut down on the wear and tear on the blade, and increase the time between sharpening, it would be of little use if you actually wanted to cut any wood.

Plane Truths for Living

In frustration, I reexamined the two planes to identify any design differences. Except for the added screw on the back of the Stanley frog, there appeared to be no noticeable difference. Finally, I turned the two planes over and compared the soles. The picture below with the Stanley plane on top and the Fulton on the bottom shows what I saw. If you look closely, you will notice that the mouth opening on the Stanley plane is slightly smaller than the Fulton's. This small difference (a little more than a sixteenth of an inch) was just enough to keep the blade from fitting.

View of the Sole of the Stanley (top) and Fulton (bottom) No. 3 Smoothing Planes

This new bit of knowledge sent me back to website of the manufacturer of this shiny new blade. There, at the bottom of the replacement blade section was a statement I had missed. It pointed out that blades for the Stanley planes needed to be thinner because the mouth opening on a Stanley plane is smaller. More specifically, I found that the new blade I now owned was .125 inches thick and those for Stanley planes were .095 inches thick. The vendor even cautioned that when ordering blades, customers should be sure to specify the type of plane. For whatever reason, the design of the Fulton plane with the wider mouth was just the correct size to accept the thicker blade.

You remember from the section where we discussed the mouths of planes that the goal is to reduce the space between the cutting edge and the front of the mouth. Typically this requires a plane with a small opening. An initial view of the Fulton plane might cause you to believe it was less desirable because of the larger mouth. However, in this particular case, the size was perfect for the thicker blade. What some individuals may have considered a weakness or a disadvantage proved to be just what was needed.

The value of imperfection was further demonstrated to me at a tool show several years ago. I was interested in obtaining a higher quality #4 smoothing plane. The #4 is slightly larger and wider than the #3 "silk purse" plane from the earlier discussion. Stanley produced a professional line of planes under the Bedrock name in the early part of the 20th century, and I was hoping to find one I could afford. Bedrock planes are heavier than most planes of the same shape and are well-designed, containing an enhancement that simplifies the job of positioning the frog.

To distinguish the brand from their standard planes, Stanley even changed the numbering scheme by using a 600 series of numbers. Thus a #3 Bedrock plane would be sold as a 603, and a #4 would be a Bedrock 604. I had attempted to purchase a Bedrock 604 in excellent condition on the Internet, but it eventually sold for over $250—way outside my price range. Therefore, it was exciting to find one for $165 at the tool show. That was still more than I wanted to pay, but better than alternatives I had seen. Perhaps the owner could be convinced to reduce the price slightly to bring it within my budget.

Aside from the price of an item, the condition of a used tool is also important. While normal wear and tear can be compensated for during the tuning process, damage that might require replacement of parts can get expensive. Therefore, it is always good to make a detailed analysis of any used tool you consider purchasing. Disassemble the plane, if possible. Check for any broken or missing pieces, and determine if all moving parts operate as designed. This should be done in as bright a light as possible.

Since we were blessed with a sunny day and the show was held outside, I was able to analyze the prospective $165 purchase carefully. During this process, I was surprised to find a tiny hairline crack in the side of the Bedrock plane's body. It did not extend to the bottom of the sole of the plane, was barely visible, and looked at first like an imperfection in the actual casting. I decided to see if the individual running the show would consider a lower price based on this newly found imperfection.

The owner was an ageless character with fairly short graying hair, a full neatly trimmed gray beard, gold wire-rimmed glasses, blue overalls, and a welcoming smile. In addition to selling tools, he teaches woodworking classes and makes excellent furniture. I have purchased several tools from him, including the Fulton plane that was the basis for this study, and have always found him to be honest and fair in his dealings.

On tool day, he is usually surrounded by a number of other prospective buyers answering all manner of questions concerning the merchandise. When my turn came, I handed him the plane, showed him the crack, and stepped back to see his reaction. He was surprised by the crack and apparently had not noticed it either. After examining it with a magnifying glass, he turned the plane over in his hands several times. You could see the wheels turning as he performed a mental calculation of the impact of this new information. Finally, he offered to sell it to me for $100. Why was there such a dramatic change in price? The small hairline crack was hardly noticeable. We both agreed that it was unlikely to impact the overall performance of the plane. The reason for the price reduction was that this crack had changed the plane's collectible status. This was perfect for me as I was not looking for something to put on a shelf but wanted something I could use.

If you are interested in purchasing a plane to use, it is worth looking for older, high-quality planes that may have some cosmetic damage. Blemishes may reduce the collectible value, but they also allow you to have the increased functionality these higher quality planes provide at a reduced price. This example should be a further reminder that Christ is not looking for beautiful, spotless (shelf plane type) people. He is looking for someone who is open to his guidance and is willing to be used by Him.

Plane Truth #15: Use what God has given you even though some might look at it as a disadvantage.

Scripture #15

"And what more shall I say? I do not have time to tell about Gideon, Barak, Samson, Jephthah, David, Samuel and the prophets, who through faith conquered kingdoms, administered justice, and gained what was promised; who shut the mouths of lions, quenched the fury of the flames, and escaped the edge of the sword; whose weakness was turned to strength; and who became powerful in battle and routed foreign armies." (Hebrews 11:32-34)

"Three times I pleaded with the Lord to take it away from me. But he said to me, 'My grace is sufficient for you, for my power is made perfect in weakness.' Therefore, I will boast all the more gladly about my weaknesses, so that Christ's power may rest on me. That is why, for Christ's sake, I delight in weaknesses, in insults, in hardships, in persecutions, in difficulties. For when I am weak, then I am strong." (2 Corinthians 12:8-10)

Application #15

The first scripture listed above from the 11th chapter of Hebrews, comes at the end of a section of verses often referred to as the "by faith" chapter. It is called this because it provides a chronological listing of historical biblical figures and reminds us of what these individuals were able to do, though faith in God. It is appropriate to use in this chapter because it reminds us that through faith their "weakness was turned to strength."

Paul continues this theme in his letter to the Corinthians. He was evidently short in stature and suffered from some chronic problem that would not go away even though he had asked the Lord to remove it. The Lord's answer was that His grace was sufficient and through Paul's weakness God would be glorified. He ends the section of scripture by making what most would consider a very contradictory statement "For when I am weak, then I am strong."

If you have what you consider a disability, do not use it as an excuse. Individuals, like planes, have flaws and weaknesses. The Lord can, of course, correct all deficiencies. However, as Paul found out, the Lord may instead prefer to take you as you are and use your weakness to demonstrate His strength. What the world may consider a flaw often makes you perfect for addressing a problem Christ needs you to solve. Past problems can even make you better suited to witness or minister to an individual that is currently suffering from a situation similar to what you have lived through and overcome.

God's "power can be made perfect in weakness" because recognizing you cannot accomplish things in your own power is a humbling experience. This humility requires that you seek the Lord's guidance and support. Like the plane with the crack, you do not bring glory to yourself but to the Master Craftsman that controls you.

Chapter 15 Questions

1. Identify an example from the Bible where God used a weakness in some individual to show His strength.

2. Can you think of any present-day examples where something you or the world thinks is a weakness has become a strength as a result of the involvement of Christ?

3. What do you think Paul meant in 2nd Corinthians 12:10 when he said: "For when I am weak, then I am strong." How can a weakness be a strength?

4. Why would it be harder for a shiny new plane to bring glory to the woodworker using it? Are you more impressed if a golfer were to win a match using a new expensive set of clubs or a set of 50-year-old clubs? Why or why not?

Chapter 16
Being Filled

Now back to the dilemma of what to do with my "silk purse" hand plane. As you recall when we last left the hand planes in the previous chapter, I had determined that the new blade would not fit in the Stanley plane because of its thickness. I was faced with a fundamental problem-solving situation. What should I do with my used plane and the much newer blade?

One possibility was to expand the mouth opening on the Stanley plane. Fortunately, I discarded that idea. Using a metal file to enlarge the opening would probably end up destroying the plane.[22] Engineers do like to look at all options, however ridiculous they initially seem, to ensure they have investigated all possible solutions. Over the past forty plus years, this approach has given rise to many uncomfortable discussions with my wife. I have therefore concluded that it should be practiced carefully around non-engineers. While using this approach, it is good to realize that not all probable solutions result in long term benefit. Remember, patience is a virtue, and one option that is always

---

22 My son and I once removed a carburetor from an engine with a pry bar having assured ourselves that all nuts and bolts had been removed. Dad (that would be me) simply assumed it was the old gasket that was causing the carburetor to stick to the engine manifold. Unfortunately, a hidden bolt was really the reason. The fact that the carburetor never seemed to seal tightly after that might have contributed to the engine fire that prematurely ended the car's 150,000 miles, nineteen-year illustrious life span.

available is to start over and analyze the problem from a different perspective.

Well, it was getting late, and I had endured enough frustration for the day. Both rationales for the purchase of the plane were no longer valid, so I turned off the lights and headed to the house. Once inside, I encountered my wife and showed her a great looking set of wood carving tools I had purchased that day and mentioned in passing that I had also found an interesting plane. She did not ask for further information, and at this point, none was going to be given.

Though I went to bed, what followed was a fairly restless night. The events of the day would not let me get to sleep as my feeble brain kept going over my experiences with the hand plane. The note the tool guy had attached to the side of the plane "silk purse" kept appearing over and over in my mind. Perhaps you remember the old saying, "you can't make a silk purse out of a sow's ear."[23] The inference was that the plane had been a "sow's ear" but with some work and the installation of a quality blade one could make a "silk purse" plane.

When it comes to hand planes, can you actually create a silk purse out of a sow's ear? At 5:00 A.M. I was upstairs at my computer trying to obtain more information on this Fulton Plane. I found a website rating the quality of planes from various manufacturers. The individual conducting the analysis of the different planes decided to take a high-quality blade and install it in a *cheap* plane and see if it made a difference. The gist of the report was that he was surprised and impressed at the

---

23   This saying has been around for a long time. The earliest reference is attributed to the satirical poetry of Mantanus a Carmelite monk. Some of his work was translated in 1514 and appeared in Alexander Barclay's 'Eclogues.' While the actual translation does not match the saying word for word the thought is the same as what we imply today. An essentially word for word example of today's saying does appear in works by others in the 1600s. When someone says that you can't make a silk purse out of a sow or a pig's ear, they're implying that if you start with inferior material you will never be able to produce a quality product.

impact of a thicker blade. At another site, someone referred to the process of tuning a less expensive plane and installing an expensive blade as creating a "silk purse" plane.

I emailed the gentleman who ran the tool show, asking if he had any historical information concerning the plane. I was fairly sure he would remember the plane because of its uniqueness. Later that day, he responded that the plane had been acquired at an estate sale and that the individual who had owned it also had several planes manufactured by the maker of the blade in question. This information made me even more curious. Rather than buy a new No. 3 plane that would match his others, this individual had chosen to spend time fixing up the plane and then installed this expensive blade.

I renewed my search of the Internet but found very little additional information on a Fulton 3709 plane. Sargent, the manufacture of the Fulton line of tools, did make a high-quality professional line similar to Stanley's Bedrock brand that was stamped with the initials VBM.[24] This was obviously not one of those. There was one listing for a Fulton No. 3 with no reference to the 3709 numbering. Used Fulton planes, in general, seemed to sell for between $4.99 and $15.00. I finally located one No. 3 Fulton plane at an antique dealer's website in excellent condition with the Fulton decal still visible on the tote. The price listed was $45, but I have no way of knowing how long it has been for sale or if anyone would purchase it for that price.

When I asked a couple of woodworking friends about Fulton planes, explaining that I had recently purchased one, their initial response was laughter. Suffice it to say, they were not very complementary and could suggest no reason a serious professional woodworker would own the plane in question. To this day, they still question my sanity when I bring

---

24   Abbreviation for the words "very best made."

up the topic. Based on their comments and additional online research, I have concluded that this particular plane was sold by Sears and was intended for occasional use by the average homeowner.

With this information in hand, I went back to the shop to see if this plane had really been turned into a "silk purse." Does it surprise you that the one thing I had not done with the "silk purse" plane was try it out to see how well it worked?

I found the two planes just as they had been left (in pieces). It was then that I also noticed something else about the Fulton plane. The surface of the frog that mates up with the blade was highly polished. See picture below. This picture also gives you a good view of the two screws that hold the frog to the base of the plane.

Front of the Frog of the Fulton Plane

A more careful examination seemed to indicate that the frog did not come from the factory in this condition and that someone in the past had spent a good deal of time tuning up this plane. Do you wonder about the unknown woodworker who evidently had sufficient funds to purchase expensive new planes but instead chose to buy an expensive blade for this particular plane? What made this particular plane valuable to him? Was it one that had been handed down from a relative and therefore had some sentimental value? Perhaps the company did not sell a No. 3 at the time he purchased his planes. An inquiry to the manufacturer determined that they began making No. 3 planes between 1998 and 2000.

While lack of availability could have been a reason, I have rejected this possibility because I doubt a thicker blade would have even been available for sale if the manufacturer did not also sell a No. 3 plane. Did the owner of this plane simply have an extra new blade and decide to install it in a Fulton plane? At a price of $65, I suspect this is unlikely. You and I will probably never know how this plane came to be tuned and equipped with an expensive blade. I prefer to think the Fulton plane had some unique value to the woodworker and he took pleasure in maximizing its functionality.

Once reassembled, and the blade carefully adjusted, it was time to place some scrap white pine (a soft wood) securely in the vise and gave the plane a try. It seemed to work well, so I began to retract the blade a little at a time, allowing the plane to take a thinner and thinner cut with each pass. Working in this manner, the plane easily cut paper-thin shavings and the surface of the wood was very smooth. Making thin shavings is a way to demonstrate that the plane is working well and guarantees that you can reduce the size of a piece of wood or a drawer side very slowly. The next test was to try the plane on a piece of harder wood (oak). It worked almost as well on the oak as it did on the pine; again, taking paper-thin shavings.

As you can see from the picture below, this plane is capable of producing shavings thin enough that you can read the underlying text. From the moment the shavings were produced until the next morning

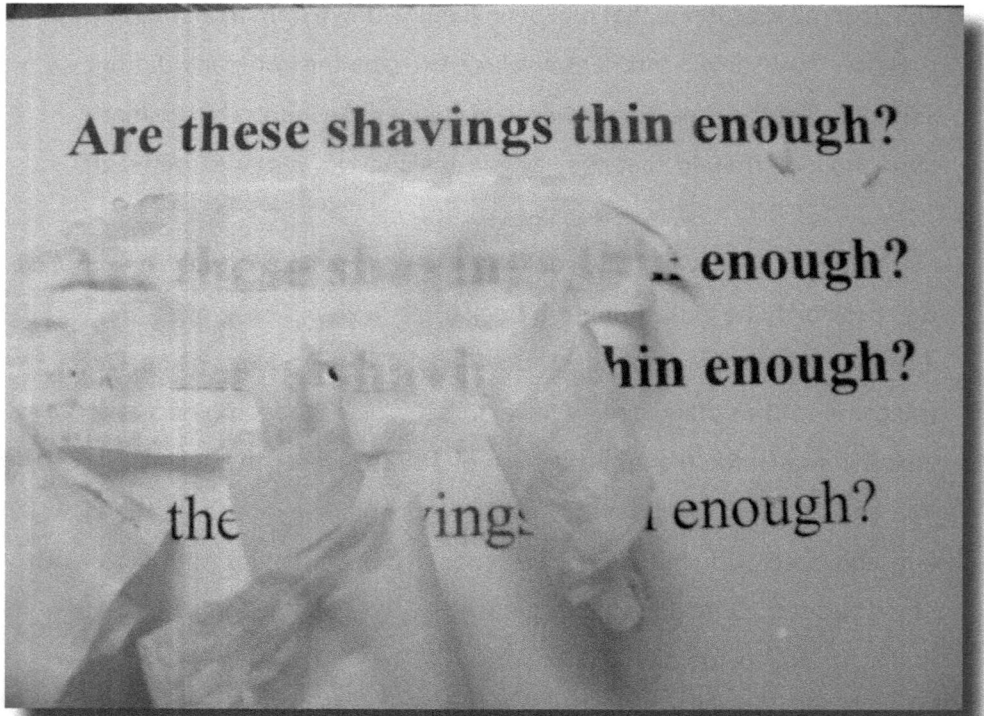

Very Thin Wood Shavings

before I got out of bed, a thought formed in my mind as real as if someone was speaking the words. WE ARE ALL SOW'S EARS! You and I are all low-end tools and, but for the grace of God, are ultimately destined for the trash bin.

You start your life with some blemishes, and as you grow older, you are battered around by the world. You receive scars because of the life you live, the decisions you make, and the situations you experience. Some of your history may be extreme and may have left you with physical and psychological bruises. When you acquire a used tool, you get to enjoy the scars of use or misuse it has acquired over its life. Again, like the hand plane, you may have more talent in a particular area than others and on the surface may be better looking than some. However, you should know by now that appearances are often deceiving when it comes to hand planes and individuals.

Plane Truth #16: If you allow the Lord to fill you with His new, sharp blade (The Holy Spirit), and tune you up; if you study His word and spend time in prayer and humbly seek His guidance, He can and will make a "silk purse" out of you.

Scriptures #16

"His father Zechariah was filled with the Holy Spirit and prophesied: Praise be to the Lord, the God of Israel, because he has come and has redeemed his people." (Luke 1:67-68)

"Then Peter, filled with the Holy Spirit, said to them: Rulers and elders of the people! If we are being called to account today for an act of kindness shown to a cripple and are asked how he was healed, then know this, you and all the people of Israel: It is by the name of Jesus Christ of Nazareth whom you crucified but whom God raised from the dead that this man stands before you healed." (Acts 4:8-10)

"After they prayed, the place where they were meeting was shaken. And they were all filled with the Holy Spirit and spoke the word of God boldly." (Act 4:31)

"But Stephen, ful of the Holy Spirit, looked up to heaven and saw the glory of God, and Jesus standing at the right hand of God." (Acts 7:55)

"He (Barnabas) was a good man, full of the Holy Spirit and faith, and a great number of people were brought to the Lord." (Acts 11:24)

"Then Saul, who was also called Paul, filled with the Holy Spirit, looked straight at Elymas and said. You are a child of the devil and an enemy of everything that is right!... You are going to be blind and for a time you will be unable to see the light of the sun." (Acts 13:9,11)

"Do not get drunk on wine, which leads to debauchery. Instead, be filled with the Spirit." (Ephesians 5:18)

"Those who obey his commands live in him, and he in them. And this is how we know that he lives in us: We know it by the Spirit he gave us." (1 John 3:24)

Application #16

How does the Lord make a silk purse out of a sow's ear? When you accept Christ, and ask Him to become the ruler of your life, you receive the Holy Spirit. The Bible explains it this way:

You, however, are controlled not by the sinful nature but by the Spirit, if the Spirit of God lives in you. And if anyone does not have the Spirit of Christ, he does not belong to Christ. (Romans 8:9). Also — Do you not know that your body is a temple of the Holy Spirit, who is in you, whom you received from God? (1 Corinthians 6:19)

If all Christians have the Holy Spirit, then why do few seem to exhibit the power, confidence, and conviction seen in those early day Christians? Perhaps it is because you have received the Spirit but are not continuing to be filled and empowered by it. Are you allowing the Spirit to fill and control you or are you still trying to maintain control? Even though you have received the Holy Spirit as a believer in Jesus Christ, it is also possible for you to grieve the Spirit (Ephesians 4:30) and to quench the Spirit (1 Thessalonians 5:19). Trying to do God's will without being empowered and controlled by the Spirit is like trying to use the hand plane without a blade. A literal translation of Ephesians 5:18 from the scripture section above should actually read "be being kept filled,"[25] indicating it is an ongoing process.

The eight verses above in the Scripture section demonstrate what individuals can do if they are being filled with the Spirit. From them, it should be apparent that all Christians receive the Holy Spirit, but the process of being filled is ongoing. It should also be apparent that individuals can be filled at one time and then require additional filling on another occasion. Part of the difficulty in understanding this concept is that we do not have a full understanding of what the word "filled" implied in the Greek language. One of my previous pastors explained that being filled by the Spirit is analogous to wind filling the sails of a sailboat. The wind may be present, but if you do not orient the sails and the boat to take advantage of it, you will not receive the full effect of its power. The first six of the eight verses listed above demonstrate what individuals did under the power and strength of the Holy Spirit. The last two verses describe what Believers are instructed to do and understand concerning the Holy Spirit.

"Zechariah prophesied about what God had done and would do in the life of Zechariah's new son John, who would later be referred to as John the Baptist." (Luke 1:67-68)

"Peter told the rulers and elders how he was able to heal the lame man while at the same time accusing them of murder." (Acts 4:8-10)

"Jesus' followers spoke the word of God boldly." (Acts 4:31)

---

25 *The Silent Shepherd*, by John MacArthur (Victor Books, 1996).

"Stephen saw a vision, and God gave him strength to speak out even though doing so resulted in his death." (Acts 7:35)

"Barnabas went to Antioch, and a significant number of people were brought to the Lord." (Acts 11:24)

"Paul rebuked and temporarily blinded Elymas – a Jewish sorcerer and false prophet who opposed Paul and the other Christians." (Acts 13:9, 11)

"Believers are instructed to keep being filled with the Holy Spirit." (Ephesians 5:18)

"Believers will know Jesus Christ lives in them based on the Holy Spirit He has given them." (1 John 3:24)

Just as filling the old plane with a new, sharp, high-quality blade results in a miraculous transformation, individuals who are filled with the Spirit, allow God to change them from sow's ears to silk purses. Through the transforming power of the Holy Spirit, you are made into something beautiful and useful. Like the unknown woodworker who spent time on the *old silk purse plane* and made it better than when it was new, God can spend time filling and tuning you. Also, like the woodworker, Christ has seen the potential you have and has given His life that you might live a renewed life. Were it not for the work done by the woodworker, and the insertion of a new blade, the old plane would have been cast aside as scrap metal. If you accept Christ and are filled by the Holy Spirit, you will be able to do what the Lord has designed you to do. If you do not continually allow the Spirit to drive you onward and be the guide for your life, your actions will be as useful as a blade-less plane.

Chapter 16 Questions

1. Based on what you have learned in this and previous chapters, what are 4 things woodworkers do to make a used plane more effective? To help answer this question, think of what a dirty, rusted plane would look like and mentally compare it to one that has just been tuned. Since you are called to be a tool of righteousness, how does a relationship with Christ the Master Craftsman make you effective?

2. Read Romans 8:9 and 1 Corinthians 6:19. What do these verses tell you about the Holy Spirit?

3. Can you do good things without being filled with the Holy Spirit? Based on the information from Acts 1:8, why do you think the Holy Spirit is necessary?

4. Will being involved in church activities, performing "good" deeds, and spending more time at the church create a spirit-filled individual? Why or why not?

5. Read Psalms 51. What caused David to feel separated from God? What does David say the Lord expects? How does sin impact our ability to be filled and controlled by the Holy Spirit?

Chapter 17

Do Others See Jesus in You?

As we have learned in the past chapters, it is important that you keep a close connection with Christ and continue to be filled with the Spirit. The last verse quoted from chapter 16, 1 John 3:24, explains that you will know Christ lives in you based on the Spirit He gives you. This next chapter examines the question; do others see Jesus and the results of the Holy Spirit's presence in your life?

As you probably understand by now, I get great satisfaction from seeing an old, misused; sometimes rusty plane returned to a useful state. Even though I have tuned a number of old planes I am always a little surprised at how well they work if you can make the sole flat and the blade sharp. I am sure the seller of some of these planes at estate and garage sales could not visualize the value within when all they saw was rust and a dull misshapen blade. To them, these were simply the items of a bygone era that had outlived their usefulness. Even after cleaning, the value is not always apparent on the surface.

I once purchased a rusty low angle block plane at a flea market. These planes are small, generally measuring six inches long and less than two inches wide. They fit comfortably in one hand and can be kept in a shop apron pocket for quick access. They are often used to round over or place a 45-degree bevel on a sharp edge of a table

(149)

top or perhaps a table leg. I find that a rounded edge is more pleasing to the eye and causes less damage to a child's head if he runs into it. Have you ever noticed that children (and my wife would point out a particular adult she knows) often have difficulty judging the amount of space required above their eyes to allow their head to clear a table top or perhaps a cabinet suspended over a counter?

I have anecdotal evidence to prove that rounded edges seem to require fewer stitches, making the purchase of this plane well worth its two-dollar price tag. In addition to the rust, part of the reason for the low-price tag was the missing brass knob where the thumb would usually rest and the fact that the blade was secured by the creative combination of a thumbscrew, and a slotted screw and washer.

In defense of my purchase, the sole of the plane was sound, and the blade was in relatively good shape. Once the bottom of the plane was flattened, the rust sanded away, the thumb rest replaced and the blade sharpened, it became a handy little tool. It still had the blade secured by screws, so it looked a bit strange and was a little difficult to adjust. I use it often because it works well and it reminds me that great results can often be obtained from an imperfect tool.

The two block planes below are included to help visualize this example. The plane on the left contains all its original parts while the one on the right is the two-dollar flea market plane. The only modification I made was to add a replacement brass knob.

A powerful example of the change that can occur in our perception of the value of a tool or instrument comes from an old poem first published in 1921. It shows that our first impressions are not always correct. If you have never read the poem, "The Touch of the Masters Hand" by

Myra B Welch,[26] I would encourage you locate a copy on the Internet. It is the story of an old violin that is being offered for sale at an auction.

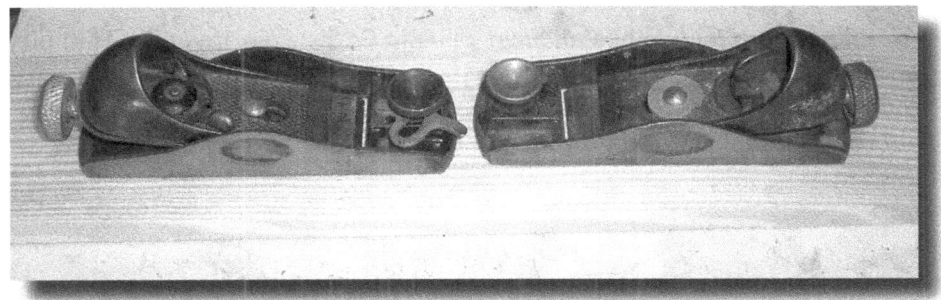

$2 Flea Market Modified Block Plane on the Right Still Works Well

Initially, there is little interest in the violin, and the highest bid the auctioneer is able to generate is three dollars. Then an old man comes from the back of the room, wipes off the dust, tightens the strings and plays a song that sounds like the voice of an angel. When the bidding begins again, instead of a few dollars, the auctioneer is asking for thousands, and it sells for several thousand dollars. The audience is surprised and asks what caused the bidding to go from single dollars to thousands. The author of the poem replies, "the touch of the master's hand" made all the difference. The poem goes on to make the analogy between an old violin and a man with his life out of tune. The Master's hand can impact a human soul as well.

As you discovered in Chapter 16, there is an analogical similarity between a hand plane being filled with a sharp blade and our being filled by the Holy Spirit. Just as a plane cannot be effective without the filing of a sharp blade, we need the continued infilling of God's Holy Spirit. This chapter analyzes the lives of Spirit-filled Christians and how

---

26   Myra B Welch, "The Touch of the Master's Hand," The Gospel Messenger, 26 Feb. 1921.

others see them. Do others see the touch of the Master's hand on your life?

Plane Truth #17: While all have value in God's eyes, if you let Him fill you with His sharp blade, you and others will be surprised at what He can accomplish through you.

Scriptures #17

"Before I formed you in the womb I knew you, before you were born I set you apart; I appointed you as a prophet to the nations. "Ah, Sovereign Lord," I said, "I do not know how to speak; I am only a child." (Jeremiah 1:5-6)

"Moses said to the Lord, "O Lord, I have never been eloquent, neither in the past nor since you have spoken to your servant. I am slow of speech and tongue." (Exodus 4:10)

"But Lord, Gideon asked, how can I save Israel? My clan is the weakest in Manasseh, and I am the least in my family." (Judges 6:15)

"When they saw the courage of Peter and John and realized that they were unschooled, ordinary men, they were astonished and they took note that these men had been with Jesus." (Acts 4:13)

Application #17

Time and time again we meet individuals in the Bible who did not think they were up to the task God had set before them. Jeremiah complained that he was only a youth when God called him. Moses argued that he could not speak and was not capable of presenting the Hebrew's case before Pharaoh. He continued to argue to the point of almost incurring the wrath of God. When the angel of the Lord tells Gideon to go and save Israel, it is almost as if Gideon says there must be some mistake. He states that he is a member of the weakest family in his tribe and he himself is the least in his family. Jesus' disciples were initially viewed by all but Him as common men.

Aren't you lucky that God does not see you as you see yourself or as some others initially see you? Instead, He sees you as you can be with His guidance and the Spirit's infilling. Under his leadership, you can accomplish things those who have known you in the past would not think possible. Do others look at you and take note that you have been with Jesus?

Think of how much better the old "silk purse" plane is at cutting wood shavings than it might have been if no one had tuned it and filled it with a sharp high-quality blade. In its original condition with an old dull blade, the time spent using the plane would have been a frustrating struggle just to accomplish a small job. After the updates and improvements had been completed, using the plane was a pleasure. The scripture from Acts 4 shows what can happen when you let the Master Craftsman fill and guide you.

We discussed God's power being magnified in weakness in Chapter 15 and pointed out that God saw fit not to take away Paul's thorn in the flesh. Humility caused by a weakness often leads us to be more reliant on God. There was an internal benefit to the weakness. The scriptures in this chapter point out that the apparent weaknesses of individuals made their testimony stronger. It was apparent to others that they could not be doing the things they did without outside help.

Have you ever met someone whose witness and actions reflected changes that could only be explained by the existence of a higher power? These individuals demonstrate by their actions that they have received the touch of the Master's hand. For me, one person who comes to mind is a friend from a church we attended. He is a stocky man with large hands and an even bigger heart for those in difficult situations. In fact, when I first met him he actually reminded me of a large gentle life-size teddy bear. He was a stone mason by trade, and I once watched with amazement as he constructed a large fireplace out of native stone in a meeting hall for a Christian camp. The fireplace interior chimney was well over 20 feet tall. The stones he had to choose from were simply a mix of native stones delivered by a truck and unceremoniously dumped in a pile on the ground. This craftsman carefully selected and placed those stones so that when the project was completed, each stone appeared to have been specifically created for its particular place in the fireplace.

When you got to know him you soon learned that he had not always been a caring, loving, Christian gentleman. As an angry, troubled young man, he had done some things that required him to spend time in prison. Once he accepted Christ as his Savior and Lord, his whole perspective on life and his response to others changed. He now has a heart for prison ministries and realizes better than most of us that no one is beyond the saving power of Christ. He spoke of how others that had known him in his past life still cannot understand the change. The only explanation possible for the change is his faith in Christ. Regardless of what others thought of Christianity, no one can deny that a change has occurred in his life. He is always quick to point out that Christ alone made and continues to make the difference.

Plane Truths for Living

The scripture verse from Acts 4:13 also shows that Christ made the difference in Peter and John. Even those who opposed them recognized they were different. The leaders could tell they had a way about them that could not be explained by their normal station in life. They were ordinary men with extraordinary abilities. The only explanation they could come up with was that "these men had been with Jesus." As you think about what you have just read in this chapter, ask yourself; do others see Jesus in me?

Chapter 17 Questions

1. Besides the scripture from Acts chapter 4, can you think of any other examples in the Bible or your daily life where individuals have been surprised by the ability of a Godly man or woman? List some of these examples.

2. Based on the verses in Acts 4, who was surprised at the courage of Peter and John? Why were they surprised?

3. Have you ever met or heard of someone whose life and their response to others could not be explained by anything other than the fact that Christ had intervened in their lives and that they were now committed to Him?

4. As you think about what you have just read in this chapter, ask yourself: do others see Jesus in me? Spend some time in private and contemplate how you think others do see you.

Chapter 18
Live Life with a Sense of Purpose

In the past chapter, we asked the question: "Do others see Jesus in you?" During that study, you should have had time to consider how others see you. Do they notice there is a difference in your life that is a result of your relationship with Christ, or must you admit that at this point you do not have much of a relationship? As you study this next chapter, ask yourself if God has a purpose for you. What are you here for?

God has equipped you with a unique set of skills and abilities. If you are a Christian, He has given you specific gifts that you should be using for His glory. To gain perspective on the topic of using your talents and gifts, perhaps you should look at our main character in this book, the hand plane.

If you decide to use a wood plane or any other tool for that matter, how do you gain the knowledge and skill to use it properly? First, you need to understand the tool's intended purpose and function entirely. Otherwise, you run the risk of using it improperly and accidentally damaging the product you are creating and possibly the tool. There are also safety factors to consider since improper use can be dangerous to the operator. If one is available, a good place to look for guidance is the owner's manual developed by the company that manufactured the tool. They, after all, have a vested interest in making sure you use their product properly. Some tool manufacturers even hold free training and demonstration sessions at local stores and annual woodworking seminars. For older used tools, finding a manual can sometimes be problematic. Where a manual is not available, you can often obtain handbooks and training videos via the Internet or at your local woodworking store.

If you have a passion to become a serious woodworker, you can even attend specialized schools where you study under the guidance of a master craftsman. These schools allow you to do more than simply learn how to use a particular tool. With practice, under the watchful eye of a skilled instructor, you can begin to learn the craft of woodworking. Of course, such schools require you to commit both time and money to the endeavor.

As you have learned from the past 17 chapters, hand planes and tools, in general, are made for a specific purpose. Using a tool to perform a function it was not designed for can create problems for the tool, its user, and the item you are working on. You could use a wrench, a pair of pliers or even a plane to hammer a nail into a board. After all, the wrench, the pliers, and the plane are heavy enough to drive a nail if you hit it with enough force.

I suspect you would be hard pressed to find a woodworker who has not used a tool improperly at some point in time. It usually happens when you can't find the proper tool or you are running short of time. On occasion, you may actually get by with this approach but usually, the time you save by not looking for the proper tool is used later on cleaning up the mess you made. Driving nails with something other than a hammer is simply not very effective. The wood will probably be damaged and perhaps even the tool itself since you can't always guarantee that you will hit only the nail as you swing your inappropriate tool.

If you walk through enough flea markets, you will see numerous tools that have been literally destroyed because someone used them to perform a function they were not designed for or used them in a way that was counter to the directions in the owner's manual. The fact is tools work best when used for their intended purpose. Like the hand plane, you as an individual are unique and have been equipped with skills, abilities, and God-given gifts. You were designed to serve a specific purpose.

Plane Truth #18: When you are able to find your special place of service, the Lord will give you a passion for the task and you will have difficulty doing anything else until the task is completed.

Scriptures #18

"Just as each of us has one body with many members, and these members do not all have the same function, so in Christ we who are many form one body, and each member belongs to all the others. We have different gifts, according to the grace given us." (Romans 12:4-6)

"Each one should use whatever gift he has received to serve others, faithfully administering God's grace in its various forms." (1 Peter 4:10)

"But the one who does not know and does things deserving punishment will be beaten with few blows. From everyone who has been given much, much will be demanded; and from the one who has been entrusted with much, much more will be asked." (Luke 12:48

Application #18

What skills and gifts do you possess? Do you live life today with a sense of purpose? Have you learned that using the gifts you are given will bring you joy and satisfaction, or do you even think you have any valuable gifts and skills? If you are having difficulty determining God's purpose for your life, speak to your pastor about taking a spiritual gifts test. This is a special written exam that attempts to identify the spiritual gifts God has given you. The results may give you some indication of your gifts. It is also a good idea to validate the results of this test by discussing it with a fellow Christian who knows you. If you have not yet found your place of service, continue to seek the Lord and pray that He will make His purpose for your life clear. To paraphrase the last verse in this section—to whom much is given much is expected. God expects you to use the gifts He has given you for His glory.

Hand planes make really lousy hammers, but when they are properly tuned and filled with a sharp blade, they do a great job of smoothing wood. By the same token, hammers do a great job driving nails into wood but a lousy job of shaping wood. This does not mean that a hammer can't shape wood or that a plane can't physically hammer a nail. It is just that the results obtained when you use the wrong tools are often undesirable.

Are you trying to perform a job you are not equipped or called to do? If you are, it is a lot like trying to shape wood with a hammer. Think back to the start of this chapter. What steps were performed to improve your ability to use a plane or a tool? Many of the steps used there can also apply to gaining a better understanding of your skills and gifts. How do you find the Lord's will for your life? Seek the Lord through prayer. Study the owner's manual by reading His word, the Bible, and listening for his still, small voice. *"So I say to you: Ask and it will be given to you; seek and you will find; knock and the door will be opened to you. For everyone who asks receives; he who seeks finds; and to him who knocks, the door will be opened."* (Luke 11:9-10)

Seek the counsel of godly individuals. *"The way of a fool seems right to him, but a wise man listens to advice."* (Proverbs 12:15)

Chapter 18 Questions

1. Read Romans 12:3-8 and 1 Corinthians 12:12-26. How do these verses apply to the chapter you have just read?

2. Give some Biblical examples of an individual who did not follow God's direction. Did they ultimately find God's will for their life? If so how? If not what was the result of not following His guidance?

3. What gifts and talents has the Lord provided you?

4. Commit to spend time seeking God and His will for your life. Read James 4:8-10 for guidance on how to gain a closer walk with God.

Chapter 19

Conclusion

When I initially shared this book in a study group, the class encouraged me to include a concluding chapter that listed all the Plane Truths to eliminate the need to flip through the book to find each one of them and to remind us of their message. They are listed below in the order they appeared in the book. I have also included a short remembrance section to help you recall some of the thoughts from each chapter that led to the discovery of the truth.

Chapter 3 - Plane Truth #1: You are called to be a tool in the hands of the Master and as such make rough places smooth.

Chapter 3 - Plane Truth #2: Rough places also occur between fellow Christians and within churches. God's word gives you special guidance in how to handle these rough spots in interpersonal relations.

Remember: Planes are great tools for smoothing wood. In the hands of a craftsman, they can create beautiful furniture. You are also called to make things smooth as you interact with others, even if you are in a church business meeting.

Chapter 4 - Plane Truth #3: If you are looking for contentment based on what you own, or would like to own, you will be unhappy a lot of the time. Strive to follow Paul's example concerning contentment as described in Philippians 4:11-13.

Remember: Hobbies can be expensive. There will always be a more expensive tool, plane, or collectible item you can buy. It is better to enjoy using what you have than to waste time worrying about what you do not have. Think of the examples of individuals with abundance who are unhappy. What did Paul have to say about contentment?

Chapter 5 - Plane Truth #4: Recognize that the Lord has given you today and you should use it for His glory. You have no guarantee of what will happen tomorrow.

Remember: Some tools and devices have a long product life cycle while others become obsolete in a relatively short period of time. Since you have no way of knowing exactly how long you will live, you should use the time you have available to be of service to others.

Chapter 6 - Plane Truth #5: As with hand planes, when it comes to your ability to serve and be of service, age is not a factor to consider.

Remember: As you read about different planes, you learned that some excellent ones exist that were manufactured over 100 years ago. You also learned that age alone does not guarantee that the plane will be valuable or of high quality. Finally, the quality of new planes available for purchase today run the gamut from excellent to marginal. You simply can't determine quality based on age. From a personal perspective, you should not use your age (either too young or too old) as an excuse for not serving or being of service.

Chapter 7 - Plane Truth #6: From a human perspective, you should allow the Master Craftsman to clean you from the inside out.

Remember: All used and even some new planes can benefit from a proper tuning. Tuning a plane consists of removing rust and dirt, flattening the sole, making sure any surface where there is metal to metal contact is flat and smooth, and sharpening the blade. Tuning helps planes perform at their full potential. Individuals also need to come before the Lord in prayer to be spiritually tuned.

Chapter 8 - Plane Truth #7: To be productive, you must submit to Christ and allow Him to file away the edge of your blade that has become rough or damaged as you struggle in the world.

Remember: Blades from used planes may require considerable work to become properly shaped and sharpened. Once properly sharpened, even an old blade can accomplish great things. Does your spiritual blade need to be reshaped and sharpened?

Chapter 9 - Plane Truth #8: Being as sharp as possible requires that you return to the Master Craftsman frequently for sharpening. Long periods between sharpening result in a dull plane blade and with respect to your spiritual blade, a less effective life.

Remember: Since a blade slowly becomes dull over time, a woodworker may not immediately recognize that the blade is dull. This can lead to problems when you least expect them. It is best to sharpen often. It is also best to return to the Master Craftsman often to have your spiritual blade sharpened.

Chapter 10 - Plane Truth #9: Keeping a tight mouth (a very small space between the blade and the front of the mouth) is required if you want to make thin controlled cuts. In your daily life, you need to keep a tight mouth or "guard" your tongue and be careful what you say.

Remember: The mouth of the plane is the opening in the sole that the blade extends through to contact the wood. One of the goals for an appropriately adjusted plane is to minimize the space between the cutting edge and the front of the mouth. Where planes are concerned having a tight mouth is important. Your mouth and how you use it to communicate is also important. The Bible is replete with examples of the problems that can be caused by speaking too quickly or without thinking. From a modern-day perspective, the Bible passages concerned with speech also apply to your use of social media and all the electronic forms available for communication.

Chapter 11 - Plane Truth #10: Just like the plane, if you get something "stuck in your craw" as my grandmother used to say, you will have trouble dealing with people and responding to others as you should.

Remember: When wood slivers become embedded between the blade and the chip breaker the plane cannot function as it was designed. Until the chip is removed, there is no way for the plane to remove wood shavings consistently. In a similar manner, if you have something "stuck in your craw," you will be unable to interact peacefully with others until the issue is properly dealt with.

Chapter 12 - Plane Truth #11: People respond best to an approach that fits their personality, or gifts and talents. Otherwise, the result could be a tear-out in some of life's most important relationships.

Remember: Understanding the surface of wood is of vital importance when it comes to selecting the correct plane and using it properly. Be sure to move the plane in the same direction as the grain of the wood, or you will risk creating a tear-out. Much like a tree, personalities throughout life can be shaped or altered by external conditions. Paul used his background and a knowledge of others to understand how best to approach them.

Chapter 13 - Plane Truth #12: In today's world, you are designed for service, not to sit on a shelf. Don't be a "Shelf Christian."

Remember: The shelf plane has no works and therefore can't bring glory to the woodworker or anyone except itself. While these planes have tremendous potential, they may never be used to serve others or create works of beauty. You were created to make a difference in the lives of others and to serve the Master Craftsman.

Chapter 13 - Plane Truth #13: Even if you are active inside a church, do not hide your light inside a nice-looking church building. You are called to get out of the box and have an impact on a far larger geography.

Remember: The storage box for a shelf plane is safe and secure. However, staying in a safe secure box will not allow you to interact with those who need to hear what you are called to share with them.

Chapter 14 - Plane Truth #14: The Lord has great plans for you, but you must not let fear control your actions.

Remember: Fear of failure can keep you as a woodworker from making something beautiful out of a piece of wood. The resulting delay in construction does not benefit anyone. When you let fear delay you from solving a problem or from acting promptly to address an issue that God is leading you to resolve, you will miss out on the blessings He has in mind for you. After all, if the Israelites had continued to be afraid they would have never crossed the Jordan River.

Chapter 15 - Plane Truth #15: Use what God has given you even though some might look at it as a disadvantage.

Remember: The large opening or mouth on the "silk purse" plane could be seen by some to be a disadvantage. However, in our case, it was just the correct size to accept a new thicker blade. What the world may consider a flaw often makes you perfect for addressing a particular problem.

Chapter 16 - Plane Truth #16: If you allow the Lord to fill you with His new, sharp blade (The Holy Spirit) and tune you up, and if you study His word and spend time in prayer and humbly seek His guidance, He can and will make a "silk purse" out of you.

Remember: When the old "silk purse" plane was filled with a new sharp blade, amazing things happened. It was able to smooth a rough piece of wood in a manner consistent with a much more expensive tool. As far as individuals are concerned, God is in the sow's ear to silk purse business. He has made dramatic changes in many individuals.

Chapter 17 - Plane Truth #17: While all have value in God's eyes, if you let Him fill you with His sharp blade, you and others will be surprised at what He can accomplish through you.

Remember: Old planes can be tuned and rehabilitated. Once renewed by a trained craftsman, people are often amazed by the results. Do your friends and acquaintances look at you and take note that something is different. Do your works bring glory to the Father in heaven? Those in Jesus' day were amazed by the capabilities of his disciples since they knew them to be lacking in formal education. They took note that what made them different was the fact that they had been with Jesus.

Chapter 18 - Plane Truth #18: When you are able to find your special place of service, the Lord will give you a passion for the task, and you will have difficulty doing anything else until the task is completed.

Remember: Hammers make lousy planes and planes make poor hammers. Planes were designed for a special purpose and when used for that purpose great things happen. Just like a hand tool, you were also designed to serve an intended purpose.

Conclusion

I hope this study proved to be valuable and thought provoking. Perhaps you have also identified additional truths that can be learned from observing useful hand tools. In reflection, I thank God for ensuring these truths were identified, documented, and hopefully remembered. I certainly had ample opportunity to miss the point. If the tool show dealer had not seen some value in the plane, he could have sold the plane and the blade separately. If I had not attended the tool show because of the weather, I would have never purchased the plane. If the blade had fit a Stanley plane, the Fulton would have probably been cast aside because its value would not have been understood or appreciated.

The next time you see someone judged by the world as having less value, remember the story of this plane. Were it not for the hands of a craftsman; the plane would have been thrown away long ago. Instead, it is now something of value that will continue to be productive long after I leave this earth. Remember, all have value in God's eyes, and you are called to minister to those that are less fortunate.

If you have not committed your life to Christ, it is my hope that this study has given you something new to think about. After thought and reflection on what you have read, please consider accepting Him and His message. If you do, you will be amazed what Christ can accomplish in and through you. If you would like further information on committing your life to Christ, please read and consider the following verses: John 3:16, Romans 5:8, Romans 3:23, Romans 6:23, 2 Corinthians 5:21, Romans 10:9-10, and Romans 10:13.

If you are a Christian, I hope you will remember these truths and teach them to others. I pray that you will become a truly committed Christian and will put these truths into practice.

Chapter 19 : Questions

1. Which Plane Truth was the most significant to you? Why?

2. What was the most surprising idea or insight you received from this study?

3. What will you do to help you remember these truths

4. In 2nd Timothy 2:7, Timothy is directed to reflect on what Paul told him. Paul said the Lord would give him insight. Do you think the Lord gives us insight based on what we see and hear today?

Chapter 20

Post Script

I bet you thought you were through with this book. Well, not quite. In discussing this study with Dave, he mentioned another spiritual analogy I had not thought of. It revolves around the fact that the new expensive blade was not originally designed for a Fulton plane. It was designed for a much newer and more expensive plane. If you, like me, are a Gentile,[27] this provides another example of how you are comparable to the Fulton plane.

The Word was originally presented to the Jews. Christ preached, and some Jews did respond, recognizing He was the true Messiah. In fact, the vast majority of early Christians were Jewish and initially continued to worship in the synagogue and in other member's homes. After Christ's death, resurrection and return to heaven, the disciples continued His work by preaching to the Jewish community. We are told that at one early meeting Peter preached, and 3,000 were added to the number of believers (Acts 2:41). Presumably most if not all of those were Jews.

The first record of a Gentile conversion was that of Cornelius, a Roman centurion, and his family. The story of this conversion is told starting in Acts 10. In summary, this passage explains that Cornelius

---
27 Someone of non-Jewish ancestry.

and all his family were devout and God-fearing. He gave generously to the poor and prayed to God regularly. He had a vision during which an angel told him to send someone to Joppa, find Simon Peter and bring him back. While his men were on their way to Joppa, Simon Peter also has a vision where God demonstrates in a unique way that some things he might have considered unclean could be made clean by God.

While Peter was trying to figure out what the vision meant, the Spirit of the Lord spoke to him and told him three men were waiting for him and that he was to go with them. The men told Peter about Cornelius' vision, and Peter invited them to stay for the night. The next day, Peter and the men went to see Cornelius even though it was against the Jewish law for him to visit with a Gentile. After hearing Cornelius' story, Peter says that he now understands that God accepts people *"from every nation who fear him and do what is right"* (Acts 10:35).

After Peter tells Cornelius about Jesus, Cornelius and his family accept Christ. This creates a bit of a problem for Peter as he now has to go back and explain to the rest of the Jerusalem church why he was visiting and eating with Gentiles. I would urge you to read the full story starting at the beginning of Chapter 10 and following. Among all the missionaries from the early church, Paul's efforts were directed to the Gentiles, but even in Paul's case, often the first place he would preach in a new city would be in the local Jewish Synagogue.

Plane Truth #19: Just as the blade intended for one plane was now being used in another, God's Salvation was destined for the Jew first and later to the Gentiles. This salvation is available to all who seek Him and call upon His name.

Scriptures #19

"I will bless those who bless you, and whoever curses you I will curse; and all peoples on earth will be blessed through you." (Genesis 12:3)

"Abraham will surely become a great and powerful nation, and all nations on earth will be blessed through him." (Genesis 18:18)

"I, the Lord, have called you in righteousness; I will take hold of your hand. I will keep you and will make you to be a covenant for the people and a light for the Gentiles."(Isaiah 42:6)

"A light for revelation to the Gentiles, and the glory of your people Israel." (Luke 2:32)

"Jesus said to them, 'have you not read in the Scriptures: The stone the builders rejected has become the capstone; the Lord has done this, and it is marvelous in our eyes? Therefore, I tell you that the kingdom of God will be taken away from you and given to a people who will produce its fruit.'" (Matthew 21:42-43)

"I have other sheep that are not of this sheep pen. I must bring them also. They too will listen to my voice, and there shall be one flock and one shepherd." (John 10:16)

"When they heard this, they had no further objections and praised God, saying, "So then, God has granted even the Gentiles repentance unto life.'" (Acts 11:18)

"I am not ashamed of the gospel, because it is the power of God for the salvation of everyone who believes: first for the Jew, then for the Gentile." (Romans 1:16)

"And again, Isaiah says, 'The Root of Jesse will spring up, one who will arise to rule over the nations; the Gentiles will hope in him.'" (Romans 15:12)

"But the Lord said to Ananias, 'Go! This man is my chosen instrument to carry my name before the Gentiles and their kings and before the people of Israel.'" (Acts 9:15)

Application #19

The scriptures above, though not an all-inclusive list, provide examples of God's revelation that His word was always intended to a larger audience than the Jewish race. In the Old Testament verses we read where "all peoples on earth will be blessed" and that by way of the covenant agreement God made with the Israelites, through Abraham, they would also be a light to the Gentiles.

In Luke 2, the theme of being a light to the Gentiles is referenced again by the priest Simeon at the circumcision of Jesus. In the verses in Matthew 21, Jesus says that the kingdom of God will be given to others who will produce fruit and in John 10, Jesus states that He has other sheep and alludes to the fact that the saving power of God was not only for the descendants of Abraham. In Acts 11 we see the response of the Jerusalem church to Peter's explanation of the conversion of Cornelius explained in detail in Act 10.

I suspect the scripture from Romans 1:16 was the verse Dave was thinking about when he told me I was missing this final truth. Like the blade from the expensive plane, Gentiles can participate in the salvation initially given to the Jews—"first for the Jew, then for the Gentile." Paul's comments in Romans 5:12 should remind us all that our hope is based on Christ. Finally, in Acts 9:15 we have Ananias being instructed by God to go to Paul, who had been blinded in a conversion experience on the road to Damascus. Here we see that God has singled Paul out for a special mission to the Gentiles.

John C. Rollins - Biography

John was born in 1948 at Clark Field Air Force Base in the Philippine Islands where his dad was building runways after the war. He moved to Texas at age two (he got there as quick as he could—as many non-native Texans often say). He grew up in Texas and received a Bachelor of Science Degree in Electrical Engineering from Texas Tech University and a Masters in Telecommunications Management from The University of Southern Mississippi.

He spent four years in the US Air Force as a technical instructor and then worked for GTE and later Verizon Communications for over thirty years, holding jobs as instructor, planner, engineer, expert witness, technical writer, and representative/advisor on numerous national telecommunications standards bodies.

He is a licensed professional engineer in the state of Texas and holds multiple patents in telecommunications. He is also an Eagle Scout, an amateur radio operator, and as you will find from reading this book, an avid woodworker. Over the past forty years, he has served as a Sunday school teacher, deacon, and lay leader in churches in Mississippi, Connecticut, and Texas. He has been married to his wife Dr. Dee Rollins for over forty-five years. They have two children and five grandchildren.

www.ingramcontent.com/pod-product-compliance
Lightning Source LLC
Chambersburg PA
CBHW060656100426
42734CB00047B/1944